KU-266-318

LEEDS BECKETT UNIVERSITY

Leeds Metropolitan University

17 0072104 4

Managing overseas
construction contracting

Managing overseas construction contracting

D. A. Langford and V. R. Rowland

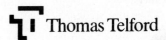
LEEDS METROPOLITAN
UNIVERSITY LIBRARY

T Thomas Telford

Published by Thomas Telford Publications, Thomas Telford Services Ltd,
1 Heron Quay, London E14 4JD

First published 1995

Distributors for Thomas Telford books are
USA: American Society of Civil Engineers, Publications Sales Department,
345 East 47th Street, New York, NY 10017-2398
Japan: Maruzen Co. Ltd, Book Department, 3–10 Nihonbashi 2-chome,
Chuo-ku, Tokyo 103
Australia: DA Books and Journals, 648 Whitehorse Road, Mitcham 3132,
Victoria

A catalogue record for this book is available from the British Library

Classification
Availability: Unrestricted
Content: Guide to good practice
Status: Established knowledge
User: Construction managers

ISBN: 0 7277 2029 5

LEEDS METROPOLITAN
UNIVERSITY LIBRARY
1700724044
B23EV
27113   4.9.95
27.9.95.
624.026 LAN
21

© D. A. Langford and V. R. Rowland, 1995

All rights, including translation reserved. Except for fair copying, no part of
this publication may be reproduced, stored in a retrieval system or
transmitted in any form or by any means, electronic, mechanical,
photocopying or otherwise, without the prior written permission of the
Publisher: Books, Publications Division, Thomas Telford Services Ltd,
Thomas Telford House, 1 Heron Quay, London E14 4JD.

This book is published on the understanding that the author is solely
responsible for the statements made and opinions expressed in it and that its
publication does not necessarily imply that such statements and/or opinions
are or reflect the views or opinions of the publishers.

Typeset by Santype International Limited, Salisbury
Printed in Great Britain.

Acknowledgement

The authors would like to acknowledge Miss Bernadette Cairns for her diligent efforts in getting the text into shape. Grateful acknowledgement is also due to Coode & Partners and WAPDA, and to Pauling plc and Dutco. Pauling for the opportunity to participate in the two projects covered by the case studies.

Contents

I

Introduction

Increasingly, the world is occupied by clients who seek to procure construction work on a global basis; designers from one country, contractors from another, materials and subcontractors from yet others. In such a complex multi-organisational and cross-cultural setting the management of the construction environment and process is likely to create formidable challenges. International construction really becomes of age in the post World War II reconstruction period although the practice has long traditions in military engineering and in the construction of the railways in the Victorian era. British engineers and contractors, Brunel, Brassey, Cubbits, etc. played a prominent role in the development of railway systems throughout the world—one British contractor alone built over 2000 miles of track. This activity was not confined to what was the British Empire but took place on all five continents.

In Europe there was major participation in the design and construction of the first railways in most European countries. Much of this work was undertaken by labour which was exported from the UK and Ireland with equipment and materials drawn from stocks held in the UK. Anthony Burton in the Railway Empire[1] records how careful contractors were in nurturing the physical and spiritual well-being of their staff—doctors and scripture readers, paid for by the contractor, commonly accompanied the workforce.

Since such early adventures the practice of international construction has become more widespread and the period of

infrastructure development in many of the developing countries prompted the growth of international construction. The
access to international aid or revenue from natural resources
such as oil prompted such developments. Many of the projects
associated with international construction are either large
and/or complex and, as such, commanded the attention of
designers and contractors from around the world. Such international players are prepared to operate outside of their home
country.

Early post war activities in international construction followed the pattern of the railway builders. Yet the very process
of development generated by the construction product added
to the process of industrialising societies and as countries
matured (it is recognised that this may be a pejorative term)
then the indigenous population were drawn into the labour
process. Moreover the process of urbanisation increases as
countries mature. Bon[2] suggests a relationship between the
state of development of a country, its gross domestic product
(GDP) per capita and the share of the urban population. This
is shown in Fig. 1. The very motive which urbanises a population and makes gross national product (GNP) grow is likely
to involve international construction. The transaction on which
pre World War II construction could be said to take place was
simple: resources and expertise transferred from industrialised
countries to those less industrialised.

Bon[3] has developed this simple transfer to accommodate
three categories of countries

  o advanced industrialised countries (AIC)
  o newly industrialised countries (NIC)
  o less developed countries (LDC).

He models the patterns of international trade in construction
services as shown in Fig. 2. The transfers from the AIC are
likely to be based around professional expertise being transferred to the NIC and LDC. This aspect of technology transfer
is one which may be a stated objective for companies. Indeed
in 1973 the World Bank[4] adopted an explicit policy of assistance to promote the growth of borrower countries' construction
industries.

Carrillo[5] surveyed the effectiveness of this technology transfer and her findings show that training and development of

2

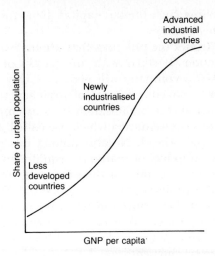

Fig. 1. Relationship between share of urban population and GNP per capita

staff is *ad hoc* and seldom is it an explicit requirement of the contract.

Carrillo records the lack of ring fenced budgets to enable a formal process of technology transfer. As it stands, necessary expertise is likely to be available to relatively few players in the construction industry and an international contractor will seek to compete by offering managerial and human capital advantages. The international firms' reputation will be enhanced by

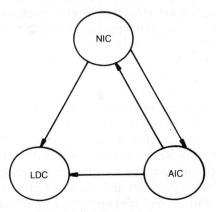

Fig. 2. Patterns of trade in construction services

skilfully controlling such human capital. How this is best done is covered in this book.

The text addresses the processes that are involved in international construction. It starts with an analysis of the range of stakeholders that a company will need to satisfy. These stakeholders will have varying degrees of intimacy with the firm. Some will be within the organisation such as employees of the firm; others will form resources which are called upon if a particular project goes ahead. Notable among this group will be subcontractors, suppliers of materials, equipment or expertise. Such firms will have a stake in the success of an international contractor and its projects.

The strength of the connection will vary and joint ventures are obviously the strongest type of bond between different firms but gradations from partners down to traditional commercial subcontracting arrangements may be observed.

The nature of the relationship between contractors from a host country and foreign contractor is often sensitive. Where recessions in Europe and the USA have drawn contractors towards oil-rich or tourist development areas then private sector projects have generated, according to Kumaraswamy,[6] 'healthy competition and cross fertilisation of technologies amongst construction organisations'. This suggests competition between international construction organisations and indigenous contractors. However Kamaraswamy also detects restrictive conditions imposed by aid agencies upon joint venturing in less developed countries. He sees a catch 22 situation where aid agencies are reluctant to give work to local contractors because of inadequate experience which cannot be gained without the opportunity to do work.

Consequently, many see local firms not only as stakeholders in the immediate project but also stakeholders in the development of an indigenous construction industry. Other stakeholders will be more detached from the firms—among them will be shareholders, the local community and the national government of the project territory, bankers and clients, etc. The function of the senior management will be to identify and satisfy the expectations of these various stakeholders. The corporate objectives will be set and the satisfaction of stakeholders requirements will be one measure of whether corporate objectives have been attained.

The stakeholders will operate in varying construction environments. For the principal players the home country will have an important bearing on how it seeks to conduct its business. Issues such as the role of government in promoting the construction industry to work overseas will be important. More tangibly, the fiscal rules governing taxation and write downs on repatriated profits will be influential in respect of decisions to seek work overseas.

Equally, the environment in which any potential construction project is set will be an important factor. Such environments carry considerable risks. One of the greatest risks being financial—this may be the fear of tardy stage payments, or even no payment at all; protection is needed against the often seismic changes in the currency markets.

The environment will also contain the institutions which regulate business in any country. Political and social risks which beset international contractors may adversely effect performance. The cultural, language, competitive and physical aspects of working overseas will all need attention. Both the home country and country of operation will be bound by an international community. This international community with its network of aid agencies, trade alliances, favoured trading partners, etc. will frame the relationship between client and contractor in overseas construction. This relationship and the contractual arrangements formed will need to satisfy the expectations of stakeholders who are centred in different environments, with different objectives, operating with different cultural stances, and with different political and social traditions. This is why international construction is so challenging— the way in which players in the international scene fit with these diverse and complex environments is discussed in part I of the book.

The second part of the book addresses the matter of marketing. While the market for construction in particular countries is not presented it is noted that the construction industry in any country in likely to be significant. Even in poorer countries the construction output is likely to account for 3–6% of GNP. In emerging countries the figure is likely to be higher as they seek to create the infrastructure necessary for economic growth.

Bon[2] has postulated that construction's share of GDP changes with the maturation of a country. As countries industrialise the proportion of national wealth spent on construction work will grow until such a point that investment—as a proportion of an enlarged GDP—declines. Figure 3 shows this relationship. Irrespective of how this curve is shaped, construction is likely to be the greatest industry for fixed capital formation in any drive towards industrialisation. The level of activity in the international scene can be captured by a snapshot of 1988. In this year 'British companies won overseas contracts which were worth over £2.3 billion and, at the end of the year, the total value of overseas work either completed or in the process of construction stood at £5.9 billion'.[7]

This work realised repatriated earnings of £700 million for construction professionals. To win projects, however, the capabilities of a firm need to be presented to potential clients. Thankfully the individual contractor is not alone and basic data on individual countries, client or projects may be gathered from specialist groups which promote the interests of various sectors of the construction industry. Prominent among these will be the Export Group for the Construction Industries, the British Consultants Bureau as well as materials' suppliers and equipment manufacturers. When in interventionist mood the British Government, through its Overseas Projects Board (based in the Department of Trade and Industry), may decide to lend a hand. It should: in 1983 (the last year for which full data were available) the construction industry contributed over £850 million to the balance of payments. In 1990 engineering consultants and chartered surveyors alone contributed £580

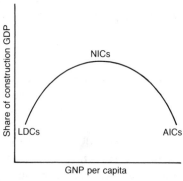

Fig. 3. Construction share of GDP versus GNP per capita

million to the balance of payments. Architects and contractors earnings are not recorded.

Despite these collective resources entrance to the international construction market is difficult. In the early 1990s some 90% (by value) of the overseas construction work by contractors with a UK home base was carried out by eleven contractors. This would suggest that size matters in respect of gaining contracts. Certainly the evidence from Japan suggests that the big six (Kajima, Shimiza, Kumgai Gumi, Taiser, Ohbayash and Takenaka Komuten) do well in servicing work outside of Japan and they are on average four times the size (measured by turnover) than the UK's top six contractors.

Nonetheless the market share, seldom a useful instrument for measuring success in construction, of UK contractors has risen from 10·4% in 1980/81 to 10·8% in 1990. This compares well with other European nations but is dwarfed by the performance of American and Japanese firms.

In order to compete in the international market firms will need to be clinical in their marketing and excel at market research to identify the market needs of a range of countries and individual clients within these countries.

Following the definition of a target market, the contractor can proceed to the establishment of marketing tactics which are likely to draw more upon the theories of relational marketing rather than the classical marketing mix of price, product, promotion, distribution and selling. Getting close to the client, often through agents, local representatives or joint ventures, is a primary task in international construction. Price is still likely to be a key qualification, however, in selecting a winning contractor—the standing orders from many aid agencies demand this.

The marketing process is explored in this section and the work is broken down into three themes: marketing strategy, market evaluation and marketing tactics. Issues of how projects can be generated are covered and comments on the way that local agents or representatives may be best employed form part of this section.

The third part of the book looks at the tasks necessary in the execution of the construction project. It begins by reviewing the project plan and how the diverse resources of labour, sub-contractors, plant, equipment and materials are procured, brought to site and incorporated into the works. Beyond the planning stage the project has to be managed and chapter 8 looks at project management. How staff are motivated, how quality is maintained and how safe working is assured are central to the text. The processes used will have features recognisable in domestic construction but there are significant differences; these are discussed in this section. The act of construction is, of course, merely a prelude to collecting the rewards of the effort and ways of handling measurements, payments, variations and claims are aired. The treatment of litigation, always a sensitive matter but especially so in cultures where a contractual claim may be seen as sharp practice, is considered.

Part IV takes stock of the process of international contracting by reviewing the characteristics of firms which operate in overseas settings. The conclusions are that increasingly construction firms will seek to extend the services they offer beyond construction expertise. The very process of international construction has implications for international trade and world economic development. Much of construction activity is small-scale and local, with fewer projects having a regional or national impact in one country. While the figures are large, the portion of the world's construction industry which engages in international construction is relatively small. Nonetheless it is sufficiently attractive to companies to draw them away from their home markets. Flanagan[8] documents 14 countries which have international construction enterprises. They are

o USA
o France
o Italy
o UK
o Republic of Korea
o Holland
o Spain
o Turkey
o Japan
o Canada
o Finland
o Sweden
o Denmark
o Australia.

Companies from these countries will continue to provide highly specialised construction expertise based upon high technology and capital-intensive projects. It is the stuff of international construction firms who are engaged in supplying materials, components or construction equipment, and combine to create projects with high added value. Such firms are likely to remain competitive for this work. Construction projects which require large quantities of labour to extract and fabricate materials intended for labour intensive operations are likely either to be the province of the local contractor or to be ones drawn from the newly industrialised countries.

The presentation of two case studies in part V support this conclusion. The cases describe project processes involved in the construction of a major irrigation scheme and a massive port development.

The descriptions cover the organisational structure, contractual issues, personal relations and construction methods. Particular problems which are overcome are discussed and assessed for their potential to create organisational learning for the parties involved in the project.

The Authors have attempted to present the text in a way which assists practical learning of how to engage in international construction. We hope we have achieved our goal.

Part I

The international firm and its environment

This opening of the book is concerned with the business environment for international construction contractors. While the framework relies heavily upon UK data, it is important to note that an analysis of the business environment can be undertaken from any competitor country and that similar analyses are appropriate for construction consultants as much as construction contractors.

The analysis of the business environment will inevitably incorporate an analysis of the competitive behaviour of others seeking to work in similar regions of the world. Competitors will be drawn not only from other home-based contractors but also from those of other nations and firms indigenous to the country of operation. Each will be impacted by the construction environment in different ways and to different degrees. What is constant is the pervading influence of the construction environment and how a firm seeks to align its policies and practices to the environment will be a critical factor in the success of international construction contractors.

Chapter 2 considers the many stakeholders in an international construction project and how the different stakeholders' needs may be satisfied. Chapter 3 refers to the influence that a domestic economy may have on the promotion of firms into the international scene and reviews the legal, financial and organisational factors which can support or repress international projects. Chapter 4 assesses the construction environment of international contracting generally and considers different sources of aid and different organisational configurations which may need to be created to secure aid funded projects.

Finally, chapter 5 evaluates the types of clients met on the international scene and appraises the risks associated with operating in various settings. This analysis is not country specific but provides a framework for analysing the opportunities and risks which may be observed in prominent areas for international construction.

The approach taken is consistent with the philosophy of the book—it is practical and pragmatic in style.

The work is descriptive rather than analytic and seeks to extend knowledge of how the practice of international contracting is best achieved.

2

Management and stakeholders

2.1. Corporate management

The corporate management of an overseas contracting organisation rests with the head office. In the simplest case this body is
an autonomous company engaged solely in overseas construction, but this case is highly unusual. More frequently, it is a
division of a group with wider interests or a subsidiary
company of such a group.

It is the function of the management to seek to implement
the aims of the company and, in so doing, to position the
company in relation to the environment in which it works and
to determine the strategy, culture and structure of the
company.

Establishing aims

A useful basis is to consider the aims of the organisation as if it
were an autonomous company. A later section considers the
stakeholders of such a company and clearly there are differences between the aims of the various groups of possible stakeholders and differences in their ability to realise their aims.

The possible range of such aims is vast and includes

• maximising the company's share value and stock market
  rating
• maximising profits

- maximising current dividends
- securing the continued commercial viability of the company
- providing continuity of employment, reward, career enhancement and job satisfaction for the management
- providing continuity of employment, reward, career enhancement and job satisfaction for home-based and project-based employees and presenting a good employer image to potential employees
- building and maintaining the company's record as a marketing asset
- providing a favourable high profile for the company figureheads
- maintaining the continued independence and autonomy of the company
- corporate growth to maximise company power and capability to resist takeovers as a means to some or all of the previous aims
- contributing to home country employment
- contributing to home country economic well-being
- contributing to the economic development of the area of operation
- contributing to the employment opportunities and welfare of indigenous employees in the area of operation
- enhancing, or minimising harm to, the ecostructure in the area of operation.

The foregoing list is by no means comprehensive. It is the responsibility of management to determine the company aims and, ideally, to embrace the particular aims of each group of possible stakeholders. In an imperfect world they can hardly avoid being influenced by personal interest and by the relative ability of each group to enforce its claims.

The balance between the influences of each group of stakeholders is affected by various factors including whether the company is privately or publicly owned, the degree of involvement of the principal shareholders in the management and their degree of commitment to the industry. While this is obviously true of any company, it can be contended that the overseas construction industry is peculiar in its range of possible stakeholders and in the triangular relationship between the company, the employee and the industry.

Where the immediate organisation is not wholly autonomous, but is or acts as a division of a larger group its aims are
likely to be subordinate to the group and its managers can only
seek to exercise as much effective autonomy as possible. A division doing well may be more likely to get its own way than one
doing less well.

In spite of the complexity of these relationships, or even
more so because of them, it is useful to know and understand
the organisation's aims while seeking to achieve them. It is also
useful that the organisation should seek to determine its aims in
such a way that a maximum degree of consensus is created and
that any hidden agenda of particular groups, which exists
outside such determined aims, should detract as little as possible from the pursuance of such aims.

The management will constantly be seeking to determine
whether the company can meet its immediate or longer term
aims by continuing its present pattern of operations, be this
entirely in the UK, wholly overseas or a combination of the
two. Other strategies could change this pattern, perhaps by
seeking overseas work, or work in a different area overseas, by
abandoning overseas work or by seeking a niche market to
which it can profitably adapt. Management will beware of
trying too late to jump on yesterday's band waggon.

Decision to work overseas

For the purpose of this book the crucial strategic decision to be
made by an organisation is whether it should seek to work in
overseas construction, or continue to do so. If the strategy is to
engage in overseas construction the decision has usually been
made in relation to a construction organisation already
working in the UK deciding whether or not to seek work overseas or to increase, reduce or end its overseas involvement.[9-23]

Usually, it is as an option of growth through diversification,
as a strategic choice in relation to risk and potential profits,
which is meant to achieve growth or offset fluctuation in the
home market. Further facets of the decision are the prospect of
greater profit commensurate with higher risk, spread of risks,
speed of growth, the avoidance of redundancies and possible
tax advantages.

A further major factor is likely to be the organisation's assessment of its likely effectiveness and competitiveness in overseas

construction. It is here that any particular quality in the suggested triangular relationship between the company, the employee and the industry may be effective. Key staff with successful overseas construction experience are an obvious potential asset and where this is combined with knowledge and enthusiasm for overseas working in key management, this combination is likely to influence the corporate assessment.

With varying degrees of enthusiasm and cynicism it is noted that very few UK contractors do in fact seek overseas work, that it is easy enough to lose money in the UK without going overseas to do so and that remaining traces of a national spirit of adventure, although necessarily circumscribed by commercial considerations, still play a part in a contractor's approach to overseas work.

An organisation's decision making process is usually, in spite of its best efforts to maximise the proactive elements, a combination of the proactive and reactive. Note is made later of the use of formal forecasting methods and an organisation will, in parallel with determining its aims, normally wish to determine a short, medium and longer term strategy towards the achievement of these aims. However the environment is ever changing and these strategies are necessarily under continuous review and periodic up-dating. In particular an organisation's attitude to overseas work may change in response to a special opportunity which may be considered as a part of marketing the firm.

To recap; central management should seek to position the company in relation to its assets and environment and develop a culture, structure and strategy to implement the achievement of the corporate aims. For some firms the corporate strategy will include at least consideration of the possibilities of overseas construction.

Within these objectives, corporate management will need to engage with several stakeholders, within and outwith, the firm. The remainder of part I will seek to review, first the stakeholders and then the environment of a company, including overseas construction, as a strategy option.

2.2. Stakeholders

Stakeholder analysis is a popular way of analysing the myriad of individuals, institutions and firms who have a stake in the

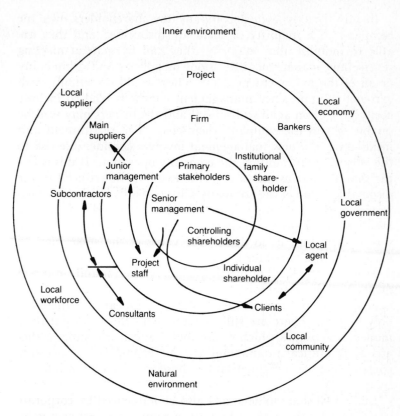

Fig. 4. Linkages between groups of stakeholders

action of the company. Invariably a business organisation is run for the benefit of its stakeholders who may be either inside the company or exist in the wider environment on the outside.

Several groups of stakeholders can be identified in international contracting. Figure 4 demonstrates the linkages between them.

Shareholders
Classically shareholders form a company, broadly define its purpose in its Memorandum and Articles of Association and recruit management to run the company under the control of, and for the benefit of, the shareholders.

17

In any directly owned company the shareholders own the company. If a majority of them are dissatisfied and they are able to mobilise that majority, they can by general meeting reverse any management decisions or policies and dismiss any or all of the management team. They would do so only with extreme caution, since management contracts tend to include costly protection against dismissal and the owners may well be unable to run the company themselves. The recruitment and installation of a new management involves considerable risk to the effective continuity of the company operation. If this is lost the shareholders assets may, in the extreme, be reduced to the disposable value of the company's assets less its liabilities which would include all compensations for dismissals and redundancy entitlements. Thus the owners can establish themselves as sole stakeholders but, in so doing, the value of the stake may be very substantially reduced.

Money is the basis of the shareholders interest and, in direct ownership, short and long term profits and the enhancement of capital value are major motives. But by no means are these the only motives. There are still investors who choose to put their money in activities which excite them (angels investing in theatrical or musical productions are one example) and overseas construction has a magnetism for those who have been infected by it.

Individual shareholders may also be influenced by corporate image and by the wish to be part of something seen as a good thing. Institutional shareholders may naturally be less susceptible to such influences.

2.3. Managers

Key managers who run the company are important stakeholders. Their work will benefit not only the shareholders in immediate and long term profit and capital appreciation, but also themselves in continuity of employment, enhancement of remuneration package, job satisfaction and professional aggrandisement.

In most cases key management are readily accepted by shareholders as joint stakeholders and in many cases specific efforts to strengthen the joining bonds are made by preferential share purchase schemes, so that management shall have a common motivation with the shareholders.

In some cases the promoters of a company become key managers and, although owning a relatively small minority shareholding, are able to continue as its effective controllers. In the wake of the recent traumas experienced by the construction industry, the concept of management buy out became popular. Not all such schemes survived, but the effect of those who did survive, together with that of share purchase schemes, is a not insignificant overlap of the stakeholdings of shareholders and management.

It is now fashionable to declare that personnel are the prime asset of a company and are equally stakeholders. Clearly they have a stake in the welfare of the company, not least in that their continued employment and income are at risk if it should fail, but in many cases there is a silent proviso that, when push comes to shove, some stakeholders are more equal than others.

Home country employees

The triangular relationship between the company, the industry and the employee is held, by many of those involved, to be peculiar to overseas construction. The company in effect exports management, as planning and instructions and also in management and staff seconded to overseas operations. Such staff are considered later but may include any or all as necessary of engineers, technicians, accountants, storemen, mechanics, plant operators, trades and general foremen and chargehands. Site conditions impose and foster relationships, closer than those in working at home, but the duration of contracts often disrupts these relationships. Transfer from one contract to another within the company is sometimes possible but cannot be relied on and previous employees often leave but return for a future contract, while a minority progress to senior management within the company. The value of this workforce as an asset to the company and identification with it by those in management with a common background can arouse sympathy with its interests and give reality to its stakeholding, perhaps different in kind to that in industry generally.

Clearly interest and involvement in the success of a project and of the company performing it is not restricted to the home country members of the team.

Local and third nation employees

Skilled staff and workforce represent an investment in training. A nucleus of committed and capable local staff is clearly an invaluable asset to a contractor seeking continuity of work in any area. A sensible contractor would seek to develop and preserve such an asset with similar considerations applying to third nation employees in those areas where local workforce resources need to be supplemented.

2.4. Local agent

The right relationship with the right local agent is the stuff an overseas contractor's dreams are made of. An agent should be at least someone who knows the local procedures, can arrange entry and meetings, can interpret (hopefully reliably) where required, ease access to local services and reduce some of the inevitable and time consuming frustrations. At the next stage the agent can provide useful reliable information. This may be no more than advance notice of a coming invitation to tender, before formal advertising; it may be the knowledge that a potential client would like to have work done but either does not know, or has not yet decided, how to go about it. The agent will expect to be rewarded for these services. This expectation and the services are both entirely proper.[24]

2.5. Local sponsor or partner

At times and in some places in the Middle East, official decrees dictated that no foreign contractor could operate without a registered local sponsor. This person is an influential local personality deemed to bear some responsibility, under the local convention, for the worthiness of the contractor. In other circumstances a local merchant could provide funds to become a financial partner or a local contractor might contribute construction capability and become a working partner.

2.6. The client and the local community

The client is king is a popular slogan; in some parts of the world it is a truism! It may mean little more than that the client must somehow be convinced that the contractor believes this. However, much overseas construction is valuable commercial or social infrastructure and a contractor may hold that the construction contract contributes usefully to local development.

Business associates
The scope of involvement as stakeholders extends further. The companies involved with the contractor in the performance of the project also, inevitably, have a stake in its success or failure. These include subcontractors, main suppliers of equipment or materials, bankers and consultants appointed by the contractor or by the client. In an ideal world all the above parties are stakeholders, working together to a worthy end. To a cynic each is to the other, part of the environment and so to be manipulated. Overseas construction contracting provides examples to support either view.

In practice there are usually inner and outer circles of involvement and influence, in which there may well be an inner circle of key management and controlling shareholders who, while owning a relatively small proportion of the shareholding, are in practice able to run the company, unless and until something happens to mobilise the inactive majority of shareholders or a potential take-over arises. Tacitly or explicitly, this controlling group will determine which of the potential stakeholders are acknowledged as stakeholders, will seek to identify their aims and the degree of concensus in such aims and will rank the aims of the various groups in determining the aims of the company.

Figure 5 attempts a diagrammatic representation of the relationships and interactions typical of a major overseas project: differences from home construction arise principally from the nature of overseas construction projects which are typically large, one-off and with a considerable measure of independence and autonomy.

The construction environment of overseas projects
For the immediate stage of consideration the stakeholders are taken to include shareholders, central management and key site management; corresponding roughly to the two inner circles of Fig. 4. The dividing line cannot be precise or immutable and others of the potential stakeholders may be included

21

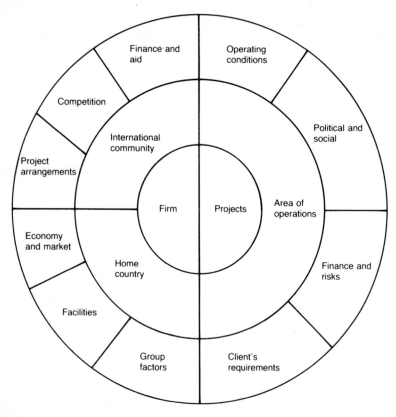

Fig. 5. Relationships and interactions typical of a major overseas project

according to circumstances. Outside this imprecise and moveable line lies the operational environment within which the management are to position the company in order to achieve its aims. Many facets of the environment will impinge upon the construction operation. Some of these are now considered and for convenience are grouped by their area of occurrence: the contractor's home country; the international community and the area of proposed operations. The home country is the location of the head office and the areas of operation are primarily, in this context, the developing or third world countries. Figure 5 seeks to represent the pattern of interaction between the construction operation and these sections of its environment.

3

The UK

The often quoted maxim of 'never work away when you can work at home' has a resonance in international construction. When domestic markets are buoyant the demand for overseas work is less frantic. Yet the condition of any developed country construction market is shaped by the national and international business cycle. International construction is set against its economic background.

3.1. Economy and market

National economy

Figure 6 offers a simple indicator of the British economy over the past century; plotting figures for gross domestic product (at factor cost to better reflect demand for resources, and at fixed prices) from 1892–1992[25] extended by later figures from the Central Statistical Office.

This shows clearly the increase in activity at the onset of the two wars in 1914 and 1939 and the subsequent decrease at the end of hostilities in each case, with these distorting cyclical variations over this period. Its most potent message to a non economist is perhaps the persistence of growth and its acceleration since 1947, and that the fluctuations over this period are, in spite of their painfully experienced consequences, relatively small in relation to the magnitude of growth.

1988/92 Central Statistical Office (CSO) records converted pro-rata to 1985 prices
1892/1987 Statistics supplied by CSO from *The Economist* —
One Hundred Years of Economic Statistics

Fig. 6. How the British economy has fared over the past century

Figure 7[27] compares growth in the UK, with that of other industrial countries; confirming long term positive growth but clearly indicating that this growth has been consistently less than the average of the other countries.

Superimposed on this long term growth is a cycle of boom and recession. The amplitude and period of the cycle have been irregular and distorted by international conflict. A stylised analysis[28] forms Fig. 8 with the comment that two of the recession phases were delayed by the Napoleonic War and World War I.

These long wave cycles are considered to be compounded by shorter period fluctuations designated as inventory, capital equipment and building cycles.[26] The efforts of economists have been directed, ideally, to eliminating the cyclical effect or, more realistically, to minimising its amplitude, modifying its period and attempting to foresee either. They are repeatedly at

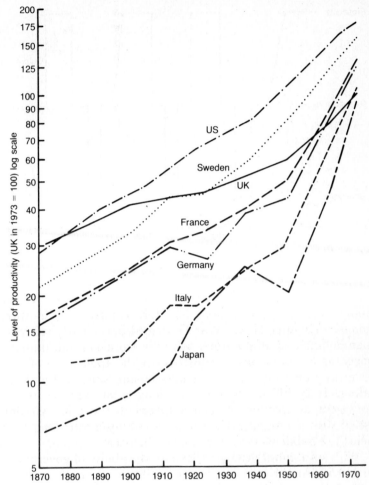

Fig. 7. UK growth compared with that of other industrial countries[27]

a point of breakthrough but such breakthroughs have so far failed to meet the tests of hindsight.

The UK construction industry is a significant element of the economy and so is susceptible to its movements and beyond this has long seen itself as being used deliberately as a regulator in the economy.

In classical Keynesian theory a government should spend money during entry to a recession, so creating employment,

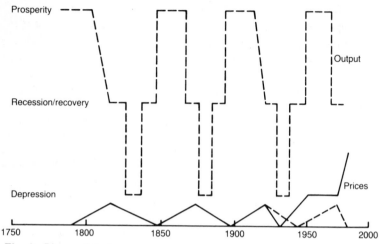

Fig. 8. Phases of the long wave

bolstering disposable incomes and reducing the impact of the slump and aiding recovery. The UK construction industry immediately after World War II seemed particularly suited to manipulation of this nature, with its workload substantially governed by nationalised industries, by the application of government regulation and by the high labour content of its operations. It is difficult to find any long term evidence of the consistent application of such a theory in the UK. As compared with a prospect of lower taxes, espousing the long term benefit of public works was not a vote winner.

With substantial denationalisation, the ability of government to provide such Keynesian expansion directly is much reduced; increased mechanisation reducing the labour content of construction, the effect of any such expenditure on employment and disposable incomes is neither direct nor immediate. Such decisions are also constrained to some degree by the activities of proliferating pressure groups, including those representing the industry and its various sections, the environmental and local interest groups.

The more general experience has been that when times are hard, economies must be made and are made more easily in construction, where individual projects are of substantial value and where the benefit of the completed project would, in any

case, not be felt before the next election. Thus when governments accept the need to make spending cuts, in view of foreseen inescapably increased welfare costs during an approaching
recession, construction projects have seemed to be the preferred
target.

Figure 9 analyses the values of new UK home and overseas
work construction during the years 1960–1989,[29] covering
almost a third of the period shown in Fig. 6. This period has
been encapsulated[30] thus: the 1960s provided long term stability with sustained economic growth; the 1970s were characterised by strategic change, hyper-inflation, OPEC (organisation
of petroleum exporting countries) oil price rises and massive
reductions in public expenditure and construction markets,
and the 1980s saw a period of adjustment, recovery and competitive change. Alternatively[10] these years can be viewed as:
stability with growth and operational change in the 1950s and
1960s, with a watershed in 1967/68 following an economic

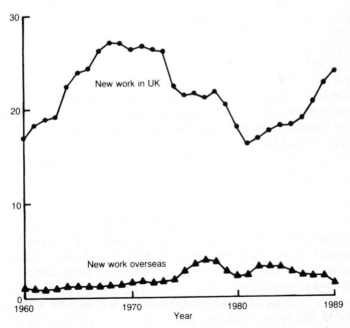

*Fig. 9. Value (at 1989 prices) of new UK home and overseas construction
work, 1960–1989*

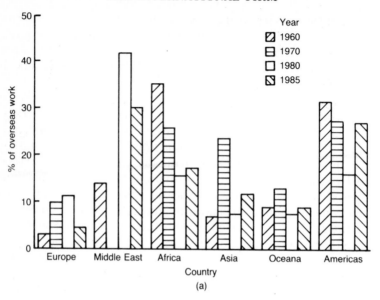

Fig. 10. (a) Distribution of overseas work from 1960 to 1995; and (b) in 1960, (c) in 1970, (d) in 1980, and (e) in 1985

crisis in 1967; strategic change in the 1970s, with reduced demand and the effect of oil prices, and competitive change, increased complexity and changed technology, with reducing workload and skilled labour shortages in the 1980s.

There is likely to be greater effort to enlarge overseas markets, when home markets are contracting and difficult, but this effect during the 1970s was compounded by the oil prices which constrained work in the UK and at the same time funded the opportunity for work in the Middle East. It is relevant to bear in mind that the bulk of UK overseas work was concentrated in the hands of a small number of firms with, for example, 90% of overseas work in 1978/79 done by 20 firms. It has been said that overseas work in third world markets during this period constituted a few golden years for a handful of contractors.[11,31] By the early 1990s the target part of work was carried out by ten contractors.

Figure 10 illustrates the changing markets in the period 1960–1985.

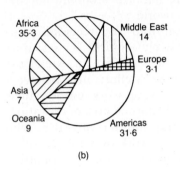

(b)

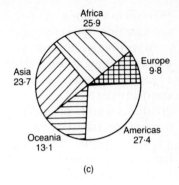

(c)

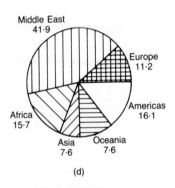

(d)

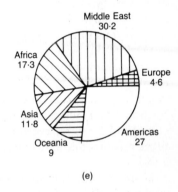

(e)

Fig. 10. (continued)

Market competition

Under modern conditions, the resources of any construction industry in skills, equipment and management, are not infinitely and immediately elastic. The financing, selection and procurement of equipment and the recruitment, induction and training of tradesmen, operatives and management all take time and cost money; and once these resources are assembled, they continue to cost money if they are not economically employed. An ideal world for most contractors offers a constant workload, or a workload consistently rising at a rate which can be matched by the practicable mobilisation of resources.

Many contractors claim that they would value such conditions of stability or steady growth above the occasional opportunity for higher profit, but as was demonstrated in the preceding sections neither the UK national economy nor the construction market present such a world.

Accordingly, during the descent into any recession companies struggle to keep their expensively acquired key resources engaged. In order to retain them they attempt to extend the competitiveness of their marketing. Such efforts may involve a greater volume of bidding and seeking work outside their normal specialisation or beyond their normal area of operation. In the extreme this motivation may impel contractors, who have not done so previously, to seek work overseas. In other cases, a contractor may well seek to buy work by submitting uneconomic bids and subsequently, if such a bid is accepted, may seek to mitigate the effects of this self imposed but enforced harm, by cutting corners in performance and/or by the vigorous pursuit of claims.

During the process some companies will have gone out of business and others will have unwillingly cast off skilled employees, some of whose skills will thus be lost to the industry generally. Some wise and fortunate firms will have contrived to contain their losses; shed their dead wood in the general climate of lay-offs; recruited selectively the casualties of other firms misfortunes and emerge, at the end of the recession, lean and keen.

However, when more work becomes available most surviving companies are under resourced and most need to recover the financial losses from continuing overheads during the period of low turnover or from uneconomic pricing.

These factors are likely to lead, progressively as the market recovers, to increased margins in bidding and in awards and, as a consequence of the temporary apparent attraction of the industry, to the entry of new firms, some of them cowboys seeking a quick killing either as main contractors for smaller works or as subcontractors.

Parallel to this is an increasing reliance on subcontractors and labour-only subcontractors[32] where contractors, learning from the scars of previous cycles and reluctant to incur costs of training and the potential costs of redundancies, decide against recruiting and building up in-house capability in all branches of their work, choosing instead to concentrate on core activities and to subcontract other work. This trend (emerging at the extreme as management contracting) is significantly changing the structure of the industry as contractors seek to avoid or reduce the financial risks arising from a fluctuating workload.

Financial market
A contractor, whether operating in UK or overseas, utilises more than one aspect of the financial market.

At the ownership level the company is financed by a combination of subscribed capital (including loan stocks, fixed coupon and redeemable preference shares) and external borrowings; the ratio between the two being the gearing of the company. In the most simplistic terms, the cost of borrowing determines to a significant degree the operating profit which the company should make to achieve a pre-tax profit and support the payment of a dividend. Apart from differentials for the risk element, the cost of borrowing is determined by the opportunity cost of alternative investment, this reflecting the prevailing market interest rates. Similarly, the return which shareholders expect from their investment, in income and in capital appreciation, is also determined by opportunity cost. In a publicly quoted company, if income and the accrual or expectation of capital gain is insufficient, shareholders will wish to apply their capital elsewhere. Any excess of sellers over buyers tends to deflate the share value and the expectation of capital gain by the remaining shareholders. Where shares are not publicly quoted, as in many family based construction companies, the shareholders expectations are similarly determined, although they are less able to withdraw their capital and may, by virtue of commitment and taking a longer view, be less inclined to sell. If a company is seeking to raise extra funds, either from existing shareholders or on the open market, for expansion or to reduce borrowing, the general level of interest rates is a major factor in defining the terms on which it may be able so to do.

The companies' borrowings are likely to include a working overdraft facility and longer term loans. Apart from interest costs, the commercial terms on which overdraft facilities are available are often vital to a companies' cash flow and its survival. Such facilities are generally negotiated to match circumstances and for a stated period. In the more distant past contractors have benefitted from their banks reluctance to use its on-demand repayment powers, although more recently others have found that the agreed period of a facility may not be inviolable as the assessment of risks, alternative opportunity and fashion within the financial market vary.

The next level of financial market involvement is in specific project finance. Here, project demands on the contractor include the purchase of equipment, the bridging of the gap between contract expenditure and the receipt of payments and financial backing to mandatory bonds and guarantees. Recently, banks have inclined to aggregate these items as equivalent to overdraft, where in the past a signed work contract and the contractor's track record might well have been considered sufficient security.

These functions are normally the field of a high street joint stock bank, using its own or in fact its customers' funds. The financing of project promotion is usually the field of a merchant bank; although, more recently, joint stock banks have sought diversification into these fields, either by setting up an internal department or by purchase of the whole or a major interest in an existing merchant bank. Such finance can be either a direct investment in the project, a facility to a developer or a combination of the two. In many countries such projects are likely to be undertaken by the private sector, in developing countries the promoter is more often a government or quasi-government body.

The financial market is essentially concerned with the availability of finance which, apart from the qualities of a particular applicant or project, depends on business confidence and reflects the cycles of the national economy and the interest sought on such finance. This is substantially influenced by government controls and the bank rate fixed by the Bank of England, by incorporating an element of inflation and by the particular risks of the applicant or project as offset by the security provided.

In general terms finance is raised more easily in times of boom and with more difficulty in times of recession. This pattern can be distorted by what seem to be fashions, exampled by lending to South America in the 1970s.

Intergovernmental aid
This is considered here as direct bilateral aid from one govern-

ment to an overseas government, as distinct from central fund international aid considered later. The basis of such aid may be

- untied: a direct payment from a government to the general exchequer of the recipient. This route is unusual.
- project directed: expenditure from the aid funds restricted to the implementation of a designated project, but with the recipient retaining the choice of the agency for implementation. The aim in such cases is to contribute to overcoming a mutually acknowledged shortfall, perhaps in infrastructure or health, without infringing the autonomy of the recipient.
- agency directed: normally the earmarking of funds to a particular project, with the requirement that companies from the donor country (and sometimes only donor country companies) shall be allowed to tender for the implementation contracts.
- chosen instrument: very occasionally, where the recipient government is discussing aid with more than one potential donor government. Then it is an offer which comprises an element of government aid in a financial package assembled by a UK bank, and with materials supply and site performance by nominated UK companies.

The overall quantum of aid is limited and the spread of potential recipients wide. There is rarely any longer a massive pot of gold commanding and rewarding a contractors' entry to a mega-project. There is also within the industry[33] a suggestion that many governments are ambivalent about overseas trade and overseas welfare, resulting in a lack of consistency in the balance between tied and untied aid.

3.2. Facilities

Government help and exhortation

The construction industry has contended, almost continually since the war, that it receives an endless stream of exhortation from government but less help than it would like particularly in overseas working where competitors from other countries receive much greater assistance from their governments. In the main the construction industry would prefer for governments to link overseas support money to trade rather than aid.[12,13,33,34]

In the UK the agencies through which support to the industry might be provided are

o The Treasury
o The Department of Trade and Industry (DTI)
o The Export Credit Guarantee Department (ECGD)
o The Overseas Development Agency (ODA).

The Treasury, in effect, finances the other agencies and substantially dictates the amount of government spending available for infrastructure and other construction works, while fiscal policy shapes the finance available for private sector construction.

In relation to overseas construction, the DTI assumes the role of collaborator with the UK industry in the pursuit of work and in seeking to direct UK intergovernmental aid to specific projects in which UK contractors have prospects or maybe guarantees of participation.

The ECGD provides insurance to UK suppliers and contractors against default in payment by overseas clients and is charged to ensure that, as far as possible, disbursements are covered by premium receipts; although recently the department has incurred heavy losses.

The role of ODA is to promote the interests of the recipient community and, essentially, to ensure that any available assistance is directed to the maximum benefit of the recipient.

The efforts of these three government bodies may thus be seen as directed respectively to the benefit of UK industry, the UK Treasury and the recipient community. The UK contractor faced with representatives of all three in a meeting is tempted to feel that their diverse efforts are difficult to reconcile particularly in order to produce benefit to the contractor.

Assistance is however provided. The DTI offers, directly and through embassy and high commission officers overseas, a wide range of information and advisory services to exporters. There is also financial assistance in approved instances in mounting overseas trade exhibitions and in overseas market research; although unfortunately the partial underwriting of major project tender costs previously given by the overseas project group is not now provided by its successor, the projects and export policy division. ECGD provides, under its buyer credit and supplier credit procedures, guarantees against default in payments by overseas clients in credit arrangements with UK suppliers or contractors. The terms of such available cover is subject to progressive review and amendment, with current terms being indicated in various ECGD pamphlets. Such terms are finally established on written application and after personal discussion. Any soft loan element of overseas supply or project finance is also covered by ECGD insurance.

A difficulty in the ECGD cover for overseas construction projects arises in the definition of default which is said to arise only on non payment after issue of an engineer's certificate. Since the engineer's independence has been progressively eroded in many areas and since, in extreme cases, such a certificate cannot be issued without counter signature by the client, this pre-requisite can, in practice, be difficult to meet.

ECGD insurance cover is also made available against unfair calling of on-demand bonds.

Other governments provide similar support to their own national contractors, leading on the one hand to accords between such governments to limit interest rate concessions and other parameters of support and, on the other hand, to a general conviction by UK contractors (or at least a general contention by their lobbyists) that the support agencies of other governments were more supportive and more adept at circumventing established accords.

UK taxation

In theory a UK resident company is taxed in the UK on its global earnings (subject to double taxation relief) less allowable costs, the difference deemed to be profit and taxable whether distributed or retained. This computation is made annually with provisions permitting the indefinite carrying forward of losses (not utilised as group relief) from one period as an offset to future profits in the same trade or backwards for three years against general profits.

Normally matters of issue are, which costs are allowable against income for tax purposes and when items of earnings or accruals become income for tax purposes.

An item of cost is depreciation of equipment and buildings. Many decided court cases and budgets seek to define which assets qualify and which write-down rate for tax purposes. From time to time the annual Finance Act will modify such terms in pursuance of policy decisions to assist industry and/or the economy.

The tax permitted write down deductions may differ materially from the company's internal assessment of true costs, of depreciation as calculated for funding the ultimate replacement, and/or upgrading of facilities and of the carrying forward of provision for possible future cost. The development of these issues is far beyond the possible or intended scope of the present work. For a UK contractor working overseas there are additional factors some of which may introduce more difficulty or more flexibility, depending on the tax regulations of the client country and its tax relations with the UK. Such factors include

- double taxation. Tax on profits paid in the client country can usually be offset against tax as assessed in the UK for the same operation, to the limit of such UK assessment, either under a double taxation agreement between the UK and the client country, or where there is no such agreement, as a unilateral concession by the UK authorities.
- tax on remittances. The corporate relationship between the UK company and its local operating organisation (which may be a local branch, a subsidiary, or associate company or an independently owned company) may be such that payments to the UK company are due only as dividend remissions from accrued profits and are, accordingly, liable for assessment for UK tax only when so remitted.
- taxes on personnel. The liability of staff posted to overseas projects to pay UK tax on salaries earned and paid overseas depends on the employees residence and domicile status, and the length and pattern of periods of absence from the UK. Since such expatriate staff will normally become liable to local taxation on earnings in the project country they will tend to assess the financial attractiveness of the posting on the basis of salary after tax. Tax paid locally thus, in effect, can become a cost to the contractor together with other local statutory contributions. The establishment of the individual's taxable status is hence of some significance to the contracting company.

Bonding
A bond in this context is a formal guarantee to make payment in defined circumstances.

Construction contracts normally require a range of bonds or alternative forms of security guarantee, usually including

- tender bond: to accompany the contractor's tender as an assurance that the contractor will accept award of the contract if his tender is selected and accepted by the client. These bonds are designed to compensate the client for the costs and delays of selecting another contractor (which may in the extreme involve re-tendering) if the selected contractor should withdraw, and to dissuade a contractor from submitting a tender on which he is unwilling to proceed.
- performance bond: required from the contractor at the time of the award of the contract as an assurance that the contractor will perform the contract satisfactorily. This is designed to compensate the client for the consequences of completion delays and for its additional costs if the contractor defaults leaving the contract to be completed by others. This bond is usually much larger than the tender bond which is normally released as the performance bond is issued.
- security bonds: for advances for mobilisation and plant purchase. These advances are provided to ease the contractor's cash flow and are normally repaid by progressive deductions from contract payments. The bonds are designed to assure the client of repayment until such deductions are complete. In some circumstances, as an alternative to a bond, plant purchase advances can be secured by a lien on the plant purchased.
- bonds for release of retention monies: release of retention monies is occasionally agreed before due date, again to ease the contractor's cash flow, with the bond providing alternative security to the client over the period until release is contractually due.

Traditionally, these were all default bonds and the bondsman was required to make payment in the event of the contractor's default in meeting the terms. In practice payment was made only after such default had been satisfactorily demonstrated. More recently some clients who were strong enough to impose such terms, introduced a requirement for on-demand bonds, payable on the clients demand without the necessity of proof of default.[35] This additional risk to the contractor gave rise to the need for insurance against the unfair calling of bonds and, as noted earlier, the provision of such insurance to UK contractors by ECGD. The premiums for such insurance inevitably become an additional cost to the contract.

All these bonds are issued for an appropriate risk related fee or premium by a bondsman, frequently the contractor's banker or an insurer, Latterly, the insurance bonding market in the UK is much reduced while banks, who at an earlier stage were ready to make a judgement on such bonding largely on the basis of the contractor's reputation, are increasingly tending to treat such bonds as overdrafts and to demand similar security. In some cases local facilities for bonding exist in the country of operation but mainly the bonding services are arranged from the UK or the USA.

Access to services
The UK offers financial and insurance expertise (notwithstanding the South American loans and the Lloyds underwriters' losses) equal to the best in the world. Equally, expert advice is available from eminent professionals and academics in law, accountancy and the construction specialisations.[34]

These services are available directly from banks and insurers, from professional consultancies, all by international standards reliably regulated by legislation and professional codes, and from universities of international reputation.

Within the construction specialities, consultant firms in architecture, quantity surveying, civil and structural engineering and the associated specialisations have largely abandoned an earlier tradition of aloofness from commerce and are generally willing to become integral and enthusiastic participants in appropriate projects.

Such services remain largely centred on London and, accordingly, are readily assembled in one place. Where they are located elsewhere distances are small.

UK is also well provided with potential associate contractors and specialist subcontractors and with manufacturers and suppliers of equipment and materials. Additionally, where particular circumstances indicate that elements of such equipment or materials are more advantageously supplied from other than internal sources then London can act as a clearing house for procuring and merchanting a wide range of services to international contractors.

3.3. Group factors

Other activities of contractor's parent group

An overseas operation is usually a division or a subsidiary of a company with other interests. In construction there are examples of UK main contractors working only overseas, although they are rare, and there are examples of UK based specialist companies providing specialist services which, by their nature, are directed to overseas work. However, in all but exceptional cases a UK contractor working overseas has financial ties to a group with other interests and in most cases has a direct link with UK construction activity within the group. The financial ties have wide implications which are discussed in later sections.

The links to UK construction interests have more specific effects. The widely held opinion that an overseas construction operation can only be successful on the back of an established home operation is not universally applicable, as has been shown by the rare exception. However, there are clearly areas in which such links can offer advantages

- in staffing: it allows a measure of trial, training and proving in the UK, so recruits can be evaluated before being exposed to the different demands of overseas working. This allows the two stages of acclimatisation to a new company and to a new environment to be dealt with separately and on the basis that if the first stage is not successful, the second does not happen. It also increases the opportunities for new faces to become known to head office staff before taking up overseas duties. It can also offer a holding pool in which staff, between projects, can be used. This capability is usually acknowledged to be an advantage on balance; although the advantage is perhaps not so completely in one direction as it may seem. Working overseas is different to working in the UK and the differences contribute to staff motivation. Staff familiar with the challenges of overseas working do not always fit in easily, or readily achieve acceptance.

● in relation to equipment: it is clearly useful to have the options of drawing plant from a group pool. Alternatively, it may be purchased and returned to a group pool after use on a project, but factors of freight and import duties sometimes outweigh this apparent advantage. The contractor may find it more expedient to hold plant temporarily offshore or to sell. Similar considerations apply to spares. Central home country purchasing and warehousing offer cost economies but again a balance of site facilities, local agencies and air-freighting may be more advantageous.

There is also the possibility of the overseas operation obtaining specialist services or products from other members of the group of companies. This may have advantages over arms length purchase and so offer to other group members entry into an overseas market which can be developed.

Need for expansion

Whether a group should or should not seek to expand is a matter of corporate aims and policy. It is not axiomatic that expansion is a good thing, but expansion may be sought for a number of positive reasons. These may include

- o to increase cost effectiveness and profitability by the ability to spread irreducible overheads across a greater workload
- o to increase profits, where it appears that expansion can be achieved without serious dilution of profit margins
- o to protect existing turnover by seeking to exclude competition from a limited market
- o to maintain utilisation and career opportunities for valued employees.[12]

A decision to seek expansion, if made, has to relate to existing workload whether this be wholly in the UK, already divided between the UK and overseas or, in the rare exceptional case, wholly overseas. Traditionally companies are said to seek expansion overseas, although not always successfully,[11] when expansion at home proves difficult. Securing profitable overseas construction work is rarely easy. Those seeking work overseas as a soft option to winning work at home have, in many cases, spent time and effort abortively in the search and, in other cases,[13,14] regretted the work secured.

Spreading risks
Most of those engaged in overseas construction acknowledge it to be a high risk operation with risks differing from, as well as greater than, those in the UK.[15,36] Equally, in the right conditions and if successful, it is accepted as offering the possibility of margins more favourable than are generally achievable in the UK.[16,17]

It may, therefore, seem a feasible strategy to balance within a group's work portfolio, higher risk, higher return overseas work with lower risk, lower return UK work.[34] This strategy offers a spread of the types of risk, for instance diluting dependence on a major UK client or single UK market sector.[37] By a parallel philosophy, the rare breed of construction contractor working wholly overseas is likely, when possible, to wish to establish some form of financial cushion by building up a portfolio of property or other investments.

4

The international environment of overseas construction

4.1. Finance and aid

International finance

Where a potential client wishes to embark on construction and lacks the financial resources to support this then either the construction is cancelled or delayed, or additional resources are mobilised. Where the potential client is a national government, likely means of mobilising such additional resources are international aid and/or international borrowing.

Part of such international borrowing could be in the form of soft loans, normally advanced or supported by another government or international institution and made at less than commercial interest rates and, as such, treated as part of, or a supplement to, international aid.

The remainder are commercial loans usually on normal market terms. Such international commercial loans are also available, for appropriate projects, to non-government bodies who are able to provide acceptable guarantees. Since a significant part of the cost of the project is incurred within the country of construction and in the currency of that country, the financing of this local cost is often separated from the international element.

When related to construction the loan arrangements may be directly inter-government or between client and banker, or may involve the participation of the construction contractor in their arrangement as a part of the total construction contract package.

LEEDS METROPOLITAN UNIVERSITY LIBRARY

Commercial loans are necessarily designed to produce an acceptable return for the lender including a margin to cover, over the spread of the lending portfolio, any unforeseen risks of failure to pay.

Where the client is not a government, the basis of lending is likely to be that repayments are met by covenanted future income from the project, or from the client's other sources and that debt outstanding at any time is secured by liens on the disposable value of the project or on other assets of the client. Where the client is a government, repayment may be from direct proceeds of the project, from the sales of other designated export products, or from general revenue, with debt outstanding guaranteed by the national central bank. Where repayments are intended to be from designated future exports, the client government may seek or instruct a barter deal. In effect, the lending banker or the construction contractor forward purchases at an agreed fixed price and rate a specified quantity of the product and through an appropriate merchandising agency arranges to convert this future right into present cash.

Massive recent bank losses on international loans demonstrate that, notwithstanding the apparent ability to hedge risks, the certainty of guarantees is not so sure, nor the calculation of risk margins so precise, as may have appeared the case in the early 1980s.

In the commercial environment of the late 1970s and early 1980s, well chosen projects found willing financiers. As in many things there are cycles and after the losses overseas construction became less fashionable as a channel for investment.

International aid

International aid, in the contest of construction, is provided to a recipient country by one of the international agencies such as the World Bank (The International Bank for the Reconstruction and Development), a regional agency such as the Asian Development Bank or a single nation source such as the Kuwait Fund, or bilaterally direct from donor nation to recipient, as noted earlier in relation to UK aid.

There can be tight or loose strings imposed by the lender. Bidding under World Bank funded contracts is normally restricted to contractors from one or more of the contributing countries of the World Bank and other international or regional agencies make comparable provisions. Bilateral aid may be given for general political reasons, as by a richer state seeking to support the independence or the form of government of a poorer neighbour or to assist a poorer nation in a specific objective. A grant or loan for construction is sometimes restricted to performance by contractors from the donor country and may be made as support for a specific project and, in exceptional cases, linked to project construction by a specified contractor.

A grant of aid may, as above, be coupled with a soft loan in a composite aid package. There are differences of attitude between individual donor governments and at different times on the make-up of such packages[34] and donor governments are naturally under conflicting pressures on this. It is not unknown for the recipients, or their apologists, to find the amounts insufficient and the strings excessive; calls for 'trade not aid' are presented from classical school economists of the donor nation and would-be contractors ritually complain that competitors of other nations are more strongly supported by the strings on their government's packages. There are consequently conventions (changed from time to time) between donor nations, on the ratio between aid and soft loan in a package and the interest concession in the soft loan element.

Agency projects

In the early post war years there was a perceived need for infrastructure in third world countries, with this seen as the prime and essential springboard to further developments. This infrastructure was to be constructed quickly, at minimum cost and to international standards of construction.

These early initiatives saw the contract documents prepared by the international agencies demanding the speed and quality of construction appropriate to developed nation standards. Cost was deemed to be best controlled by open competitive tender. Frequently bids were confined to firms whose base was in the same country as the host agency. This approach to construction in the developing world may now be thought simplistic, but it did achieve its immediate objectives and also fostered the renaissance of international construction.

IBRD[38] have noted their efforts since the mid 1970s to foster local construction industries and it is noticeable that there was little such effort before this.

4.2. Competition

While the data for this section has been drawn from the UK the arguments can be international in that the important characteristic is the relationship between the contractor's home country and the country of operation of the international project. The areas of operations for UK contractors are the subject of subsequent chapters. From the immediate post war period until the mid 1960s, the UK overseas construction industry operated generally in what was an extended domestic market in the sterling area, in colonies or former colonies. From the late 1960s a pattern developed of intense competition between developed nation contractors for work in developing nations centred in the 1970s on the Middle East oil boom.[10,30,39]

In the late 1970s, as noted later in relation to areas of operation, new competition entered the international market by third world contractors developing in their home markets and subsequently seeking to export their activity. The decline in Middle East demand and the general tightness of funding for construction in developing areas, together with this increased availability of potential contractors, has led naturally to intense and sometimes uneconomic competition.

International corporate acquisition

The increasing internationalisation of business in recent decades has produced a major effect on the distribution and nature of UK overseas·construction. The figures are stark, and some snapshots help to measure the turbulence of the market. In 1977/78 and 1978/79 the Middle Eastern overseas activity by contractors constituted some 50% of total international output. By 1990 this had fallen to 5% of total activity. Between 1978/79 and 1980/81 some £350 million worth of work had vanished in the Middle East.

Conversely, in the same period output conducted by UK firms mostly in the Americas grew from £127 million (10% of the total) in 1977/78 to £957 million (47% of the total) in

1990. These data are not indexed to a particular year since inflation will vary over the years and will occur at different rates in different parts of the world.

This reported expansion in America is largely the product of the formation of companies in the USA or purchase of, or into, existing US companies supported by local resources of materials, equipment and management.

Whereas traditional international construction contracting markets contributed to home country employment and materials and equipment supply, the new ones were largely autonomous. In essence the home country contractor contributes money, top management and key personnel and if the venture succeeds, takes out money and some knowledge.

4.3. Project arrangements

Contract arrangements

In the early part of this period the contractual arrangements were typically unrestricted tender. The simplified case for this type of contract was that the client would generally obtain the lowest bid price and that it was then the function of the conditions of contract, programme and specification to ensure time and quality. However, in international construction as in domestic, there has been an increasing recognition that the lowest price may be uneconomic.[30,33,34,40-42] It may have come simply from the estimator who made the biggest mistake, from a cowboy bidding recklessly or from a local contractor confident that he will be bailed out if his bid against foreign competition should prove loss making.

No matter what the document may say, it is very often difficult to enforce high performance and quality standards and ensure against corners being cut by a contractor. Even more so with one who is losing money; it is usually impossible with an incompetent contractor who is losing money.

Tenders, particularly international tenders, are costly to produce. The cost of unsuccessful tenders must, across the board, be recovered in successful bids and a contractor will often choose not to bid if the foreseen list of bidders is too long and, particularly, if it seems to include those likely to submit reckless and uneconomically low bids. This process may thus discourage and exclude the contractors the client would wish to appoint for the work.

While tender invitations almost invariably state that the lowest bid may not be accepted, to do otherwise leaves the awarding authority open to questions of probity. The adjudicator may well have no personal responsibility for subsequent performance of the work and the less risky path of accepting the lowest bid is often followed even against the advice of the client's own technical officers and consultants. If the choice is unwise the reckoning comes later.

Over the years the force of such arguments has been acknowledged. One extreme alternative system adopted was to invite bids by percentage above or below the client's estimate, to discard the highest and lowest bids, to take the average of the remaining bids and to award the contract to the bidder closest to the average figure. The apparent reasoning was that the average figure would eliminate errors in tendering and approximate to the right economic price for the work and that a contractor receiving this price could afford to, and so could be compelled to, give good performance.

The less extreme alternative frequently adopted is to restrict bidding to contractors invited to tender after pre-qualification.

Such pre-qualification is normally based on the client's or his consultant's previous knowledge of the contractor or on the contractor's response to a published invitation to seek to pre-qualify, and submission of particulars of his experience and financial equipment and technical resources. This at the same time reduces the number of bidders and thus the abortive costs of unsuccessful bids, and gives some assurance of the competence of those contractors invited to bid. In a less than perfect world, however, the list issued is not always sacrosanct and there are sometimes subsequent and less well chosen additions to the list for political or other reasons.

A good theoretical case could be made for grading bidders on their pre-qualification information, past record and the technical content of their bid submission. A weighting factor by which the bid price would be multiplied could be derived from this grading; the excess of the weighting factor over unity representing a provision for potential additional cost in supervision, delays, remedial work and claims, associated with a less than perfect contractor. This would seem to reflect the informal process by which the choice between a higher and lower bid is made, usually in much smaller contracts, where the individual making the choice has complete authority and will be responsible for the success or failure of subsequent performance. Its application in practice to major contracts is more difficult.

Local participation

The extent of local participation depends on the political will to promote it and on local capability. Such participation can be as financial promoter and controller of the work, as main contractor, as subcontractor and as individual employee.

Earlier the prime perceived aim was the cost effective and timely completion of the construction works required. The advantages of parallel development of local capacities and of local construction industry were not then issues of significant international concern. However, progressively it was suggested that it might be more appropriate to adapt designs to enable the maximum use of local resources (rather than imported technology and equipment) and to promote the direct involvement of local contractors.[36,38,43–45]

5

The area of proposed operations

5.1. Clients' requirements

Regions

The changes in the market for construction services in third world and developing countries since the war are extensively recorded in the housing and construction statistics. Three distinct stages in market development can be identified. Immediately post war (1949–1955) the work was focused upon the sterling area: Canada, Australia, Central and Southern Africa. In the late 1960s and early 1970s the work had shifted to former colonies (be they of the UK or other European powers). By the late 1970s and 1980s the Middle East was the principal recipient of construction work.[10,18,39,46,47]

In the mid 1980s with the decline in the Middle East markets attempts were inevitably made to foresee the next major area of opportunity; the favourites at the time seeming to be the Far East, South America and China.[35] In the intervening years it can probably be said that none of these three areas has met these expectations. On work in the Far East only Hong Kong has grown as a market; the rest of Asia shrunk from a market of just over £300 million in the 1980s to just over £100 million in 1990.

Corresponding expectations in South America were submerged, at least for a time, in the banks' repayments crisis while China continues to be impossible to ignore, but expectations are still largely in the future. Some 80 years ago a UK contractor wrote 'During the past 20 years we have been striving to get work in China, with practically no return. But contractors are patient people, and we wait, even if we do not see'.[48] A century is perhaps little in the Chinese timescale.

Data presented by Harvey and Ashworth (1993)[49] is shown in Fig. 11 and emphasises the downturn in world construction in the latter part of the 1980s. The salient exception is the American market which provided the market for the changed emphasis in overseas work carried out by UK contractors.

Attempting to anticipate future markets is a key aspect of competition in international construction. Many construction organisations have used formal forecasting methods such as Delphi techniques and scenario planning to explore the changes which propel shifts in trading conditions. A contemporary *tour d'horizon* would see the Middle East as immensely rich and the expanding world demand for energy suggests that oil revenues are not yet a matter of history. The spread of infra-

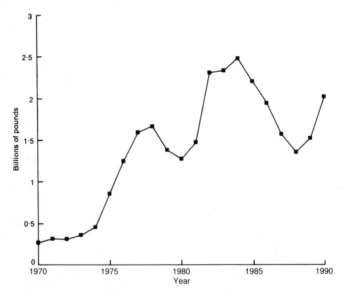

Fig. 11. Overseas construction by UK contractors

structure construction has not been even, Iraq and Iran have much to make good.

The third world countries are seen to be stratifying; with the poorer nations, predominantly in Africa, continuing to have to rely on world funding for infrastructure development. This, over the past decade, has been less readily available. The next strata of nations, including much of South America, are developing economies which can attract international investment. This not only generates its own construction demand but can also fund the financial base for necessary infrastructure.[50]

Throughout Asia some economies are developing at rates significantly greater than those of the developed world. As demand for construction services increases the indigenous capability to meet these demands grows.[51]

To these areas there must be added in the immediate future the newly independent nations of the former Soviet block— with potential for economic expansion indisputable when politically realisable—the Indian subcontinent with its vast resources of human talent and always China.

The possibilities of the European Union (EU) and of continuing development of the industry similar to the recent expansion by investment in the Americas provide an environment pregnant with prospects for overseas contractors.

Need for construction
The contributions which construction can make to development are widespread and fundamental and would seem to be indisputable. They include roads, railways, ports and airports as the basis of communications and distribution; irrigation and flood control, water supply and treatment; factories and equipment for industry and the building and equipment needs of housing, schools and hospitals.

A demand for construction has two essential elements; a desire for the project, which may or may not reflect a real need, and the financial resources to pay for it. Many contractors would add further elements and contend that there is little difficulty in identifying an area where construction works are both wanted and needed. Two further requirements are that the potential client should have, or be able to procure, the funds for payment, and that the contractor can expect to be duly paid in a form which it can convert and remit.

There is an overlap between need and desire. It has been said that no client really wants a construction project; that what it wants is the productive use of the finished product, with the project itself merely a nuisance and a delay. This makes sense in commercial terms, but in political terms there may be advantages in being seen to be doing something and there are often political pressures to pursue a project deemed likely to be popular with one section or another of the community. This is sometimes reflected in an artificial timing of such work so that its commencement or commissioning occur at a favourable time in relation to an election or other relevant event.

Indisputably there have been examples of undue extravagance in overseas construction,[52] but this does not occur only in palaces in the Middle East; other examples can be sited such as international banks in London.

There is an on-going cry to be seen to be eliminating grandiose schemes so as to give due importance to social provisions such as housing, water supply, schools and hospitals. Decision makers need to exercise choice between competing schemes in this context.[53] The selection of projects using techniques such as cost benefit analysis may be superficially attractive. However, there is little unanimity on the evaluation of tangible, intangible and environmental benefits in comparable units, nor is it always easy to persuade the local participants, be they paymaster or aid recipient, that the evaluation is inevitably and eternally correct.

Earlier, the status of the client as a stakeholder in a construction project was considered; Fig. 4 is drawn on the some are more equal than others principal, showing the client as outside the inner core of stakeholders. Later in relation to marketing the need for a contractor to identify with the client will be considered and, it is appropriate to note at this stage, that the degree of identification with the client is a major element in the project environment. That is exemplified by two particular sets of circumstances: in the first, the client is the benevolently autocratic ruler of a small state where the contractor has, and wishes to maintain, a continuing presence; in the second, the contractor is involved with the client in project creation. In these and in other less extreme cases the contractor needs to know and take account of the client's requirements; and to at least give a convincing appearance of commitment to these requirements.

It has been suggested[32] in relation to the UK industry, that a client wants minimum disruption, a finished facility to meet his needs, completion to time, cost and quality and life cycle value for money, plus protection from cowboys, with one reference point, but with the right to interfere and change its mind. Alternatively, it has been suggested that the requirements of a typical overseas client, by implication an overseas government or similar, include the creation of employment, protection of foreign exchange reserves, national prestige and strategic or defence needs.[35] This already offers a sufficiently wide spectrum of need but there are many further varieties of client, be they in the government or private sector. The motives of clients may be further complicated by clients being dependent upon an electorate or other body of support and so wishing to give the appearance of being seen to do the popular thing, at the favourable time. The political dimensions of the project selection process complement the popularity (or otherwise) of the completed facility.

A further important element is a requirement for advice on project selection.[19,47] The provision of such advice may be primarily the role of a consultant. The advice of the consultant may carry great weight in settings where the client's technical staff are relatively unsophisticated and the relationship between the contractor and the appointed consultant may be critical in settings where project creation is sought. Additionally, the relationship between the contractor and client is crucial, and inevitably conditioned by the degree to which the contractor does or does not accept the client as a stakeholder in the project. This relationship has a bearing on the client's requirements, on the client's appreciation of its own requirements and on the contractor's response to these requirements.

At its simplest the meeting of the client's requirement is the purpose of the project. Few things are simple in international construction, the client's advisers (sometimes in conjunction with the contractor) may have their own agendas and motivations which add to or detract from the satisfaction of client requirements. The political management of the coalition of interests can become a central element of project management.

Consultants

Design consultants may be simply selected by the client directly, or on the contractor's recommendation or nominated by an international agency or aid donor. Alternatively, design consultants may be integrated with the contractor to provide a design/build service. The traditional contract arrangement will begin with the preliminary and feasibility studies and continue through the stages to final design, tendering and award of contract. These will precede supervision of construction, final measurement and settlement of contract. Alternatively, feasibility study, design and supervision may be treated as separate stages and entrusted to different consultants, although, since some measure of design revision during construction is usually required, there may well be some dispute on design liability if this route is followed.

Occasionally, a consultant is imposed on the client by a stated or implied condition of an aid package. In such circumstances the design consultant is chosen to provide assurance to the donor that the aid money is being properly spent. Additionally, such arrangements give assurance to potential contractors of impartiality in the administration of the contract. In these circumstances the choice of consultant is likely to be from an established circle of international names from North America or Western Europe. It is likely, as a matter of policy, to exclude consultants from the country in which the project is to be performed. In other cases a donor government may seek the appointment initially of a consultant and subsequently of a contractor from its own country.

Where the consultant effectively comes with the contractor there are potential advantages in relation to value engineering but there are also potential difficulties of real or apparent conflict of interest and responsibility. In such circumstances it has been the practice of UK consultants to perform work to the design stage under an association with the contractor. Involvement thereafter being subject to a separate contract with the client but with the costs of such a contract usually coming within the general project funding package.

Where the client chooses its own consultant, it may choose from the established circle of international names or select a consultant from its own country. Design consultants are involved increasingly in marketing their services.

The consultant is a major feature of the project environment. At the design stage it vitally influences the buildability of the project, in supervision it similarly influences the acceptance or rejection of work and the certification of measurement for payment. Most contractors, if asked, would claim to prefer a strong consultant implementing the contract fairly and independently and with the ability to resist undue interference by the client.

5.2. Finance and risks

Economy

The state of the national economy of the country of operation clearly has a widespread impact upon a construction project. Earlier comments on the potential of different regions of the third world to provide work underline this.

The state of any economy depends upon the combination of access to basic resources, political decisions about the distribution of these resources and economic management.[50] In certain conditions the access to basic resources may dominate other factors, the oil resources of the Middle East is an obvious example. At the other end of the spectrum are those countries with few known material resources and desperately underdeveloped human resources which, consequently, are unable to attract inward commercial investment and remain to a large degree dependent upon international aid funding.

The national economy may be substantially based on a single export product, oil as noted above, but also food products or raw materials. It may be dependent on the continued remittances of its nationals working overseas or on continuing overseas aid. It may be internationally creditworthy or already burdened with excessive debt.

If the project is internally government financed, the national economy determines the client's eventual ability to pay; either in negotiable currency or in goods of trade. Payments may be tardy if the government runs into economic difficulties. The national economy may also impact the promptness and reliability of payment by a private sector client. In the case of an externally aided project actual payments to the contractor may be insulated from the national economy. However, the state of the economy has impacts beyond the simple issue of contract payments; it will certainly shape the local working environment. For example, if the economy is basic there is likely to be a shortage of skills and few manufactured products, although labour, basic foods and raw materials may be readily available and inexpensive.

The condition of the economy is also a major factor in the motivation of the parties who initiate the project. Projects which will, directly or indirectly, satisfy an urgent human need for say food or shelter are likely to attract funding from national or international agencies.

In construction such projects are likely to be based upon infrastructure development which enables measures to alleviate chronic need to take place. A thriving economy provides the basic wealth which can then fund either government or private sector initiatives and, at the same time, provide the necessary confidence to make possible offshore borrowing and to invite offshore investment. The condition of the economy further compounds these factors by its influence on the terms on which those seeking to work or invest in the country can insure against risks.

There are a few projects which can be self financing within a short term and with a minimum of risk, and can, on this basis and given the political will, be virtually isolated from the national economy.

Illustrative examples could be road and/or rail infrastructure facilities providing access to an extraction operation for a mineral internationally in demand, paid for under a barter deal by a 'first call' on part of the mineral extracted; or, similarly, access, irrigation and processing facilities for an agricultural crop internationally in demand paid for by a first call on the crop.

Those exceptional individual projects which are sufficiently self financing and which can by political will be kept virtually self contained, can proceed virtually independent of the condition of the local economy. Obviously such projects interact with the local economy in as much as local services, labour, etc. are purchased from it. The early days of oil development in the Middle East and the more recent days of mineral development in Papua, New Guinea are examples of such projects.

External finance

External sources of finance include the product of international trade and remittances of nationals working overseas, but are here considered as international investment or commercial loans or international or intergovernmental aid.

As noted in the preceding section, with the exception of projects which are over a relatively short period self financing, international investment and the possibility of offshore commercial loans depend substantially on the strength of the national economy and, particularly, on the degree of international confidence in its strength. Given such confidence, international investment becomes possible and it also becomes possible for national firms seeking to expand to establish satisfactory guarantees and to borrow on international markets. International suppliers can also obtain financial cover for their transactions. Such development is likely to involve a need for private sector construction.

International or intergovernmental aid may be provided as a booster to countries which, by their own efforts, are making some progress in development. Aid agencies are amenable to the concept of mixing national and aid funds to enable a project to get underway.[50]

Such aid may be channelled through one of the United Nations development funds or through one of the parallel regional funds for development. Routeing aid in this way insulates the project from political implications.

Taxation

The position of UK taxation in relation to overseas contracts was considered earlier but local taxation is also a prime concern. The Authors do not intend to try and review the taxation arrangements of all countries where international construction takes place. The subject can only be treated cursorily and in relation to how it impinges upon the operation of an overseas construction project in general. Taxation is, however, of vital importance to a contractor in relation to the viability of a project and when considering entry to a new work area.

Taxes, duties, levies, contributions or equivalent statutory imposts are charged by the government of many of the countries of operation and sometimes additionally by regional bodies within the country.

Such imposts can include

- charges on any or all of company turnover, profits or off-shore remittances. There is often a withholding tax on remittances of contract income from the host country. This is nominally as an on-account payment to be adjusted against later assessment of tax on profit, but in practice sometimes operates as a practical alternative to direct tax assessment.

  Many countries operate with low percentage capital allowance write downs of initial plant costs in substitution for realistic discounts depreciation and impose severe restrictions on, or total deletion of, the accounting charge for head office overheads.

- charges on the wages, salaries, allowances and benefits paid to local and expatriate employees. As noted earlier, where expatriate employees are involved the yardstick by which they judge the attractiveness of the renumeration package is usually the net of tax, remittable element.

  In countries where local earnings are low, expatriate salaries become liable to the penal higher bands of local income tax and this cost may be considerable. In some cases offshore payment of inducement allowances or performance rewards may be permitted with the effect of reducing such tax costs. In other cases payroll taxes, or welfare, or similar payments will need to be paid by the employer.

- charges on the import of materials, equipment and spares. These appear in various guises and may be compounded with port dues and other charges. They may sometimes be designed to protect a local industry, but may in practice be applied, still at high levels, to items the local industry cannot or does not produce.

- charges on the extraction of raw materials and on the transfer of materials across regional boundaries within the country. The extraction charges may be assessed as a royalty on the quantity of material extracted or as a permit charge related to the area to be worked. Boundary charges in turn may be on the weighed quantity, or declared value of material moved, or on the number of truck crossings.

- charges for a specific social or national purpose. These may be levies for a campaign against illiteracy, or particular diseases, or perhaps a national defence fund contribution.

In many developing nations, the definitive legislation governing such charges has failed to keep pace with their application, leaving a margin of uncertainty or flexibility in their impact. It is almost always essential to have local advice and guidance on the practical application of such charges despite its not always being easy to evaluate the quality and reliability of such advice. An adviser may offer a low assessment of payments to be made and charge a substantial fee on this basis; with the assessment subsequently found to be grossly underestimated.

In some cases there is international relief from the impact of local charges. The principal example is double taxation relief, where the contractor's home government, either by reciprocal arrangement with the country of operations, or unilaterally, will offset tax paid in the country of operations against tax otherwise payable at home. Where such taxes are on a comparable basis the contractor pays the higher of the two charges. There are also tax exemption clauses in some internationally aid funded projects, where the aid donors are unwilling to fund the cost of local taxes in addition to those of the project and negotiate such an exemption clause as a condition of aid.

Additionally, there are sometimes financial inducements, such as reduced tax rates or tax holidays, offered to overseas operators or investors to encourage the establishment or expansion of a local industry.

Exchange rates and controls

A contractor operating overseas needs internationally negotiable currency for the funding of various aspects of project performance. These include the purchase offshore and import of project materials and equipment; the remitting by expatriate staff of any savings from salaries paid locally, and the remitting by the contractor from its external earnings of a contribution to home overheads and of its profit.

If the currency of the country of operation is uncontrolled and internationally acceptable for exchange, the prime issue becomes one of stability of the exchange rate. The contractor, if fortunate enough to have liquid assets, may as a matter of its corporate treasury control choose to hold these in a spread of currencies, hoping for protection against individual rate changes. It may also buy forward, agreeing to pay a predetermined rate, at a foreseen future date, when a particular currency will be required for the purposes of the project. While the risks leading to such precautions have, for a long time, been a part of contracting in the third world, such transactions are not trouble free. Indeed much of the lobbying for a common EU currency seems to come from businessmen anxious to eliminate such problems in their transactions within the EU.

If there are exchange controls and/or a weak local currency not internationally accepted and thus volatile in conversion, a new set of conditions comes into play. There may be a single but fluctuating exchange rate in which case necessary funds for an international project are normally eligible for exchange at the rate prevailing when converted. This does not mean, however, that there will be no payment delays. These can arise simply due to bad administration, or may be caused or increased by an underpaid junior official seeking an inducement to cause matters to move more quickly.

There may be, however, more than one rate of exchange; possibly, simply an official rate and a black rate in an unofficial market which may, or may not, be tolerated. Alternatively, there may be more than one official rate; a basic exchange rate and a premium rate favouring the external currency available on special permit for prescribed purposes. Any of these additional conditions inevitably serve to compound the difficulties and delays of the single rate system.

The terms of international contracts, particularly those with government clients, often include provisions aimed to reduce such difficulties. Mobilisation and plant purchase advances are intended to reduce the financial injection which the contractor has to make to the project. Provisions for payments of advances in a specified international currency, at an exchange rate fixed in the contract, are designed, as far as possible, to transfer the risk on exchange rate from the contractor to the government client. Such advances are frequently recovered in instalments against payments due for work measured and certified by the supervising consultants.

Risks

It has been suggested that overseas work offers to a contractor the prospect of greater profit commensurate with greater risk.[17] From another viewpoint there are risks on both sides and the person signing the contract may be staking reputation, job, or neck on the contractor's ability to deliver.[35]

Essentially, all the aspects of the environment of the country of operation present some element of risk either to the contractor's finances, or reputation, or to the well-being of his staff. Some risks are common to construction contracting, whether in the UK or overseas, but the elements emphasised here are those where there are differences between work in the UK and work overseas. It has been claimed that you get a better class of ulcer working overseas.

There are potentially physical risks to staff. Climate can cause problems, health provisions, and site health and safety standards may not match those of the UK. There are, from time to time, risks of working in areas of war or civil disturbance, or outside the effective control of law and order enforcement. There are also, in some cases, risks of political sequestration of equipment, or other assets, or detention of staff.

Other risks may relate to project performance; delays in providing necessary permits and licenses can cause set-backs. Site access, or the provision of facilities, or poor performance by local labour, subcontractors or suppliers can lead to delay.

Such delays add to the financial risks. The costs of dealing with such occurrences, of making good defective work or materials, the costs of extended working periods or those of making good delays have to be accounted for. There are also possible financial problems from delayed payments or from the clients' failure or inability to make payment and the implications of exchange controls and exchange rates.

In the natural order of things there are measures aimed to provide some protection to the contractor from some of these risks. These are written into the contract and include risk sharing.

Standard contract conditions include provisions for additional payment to the contractor in relation to costs arising from specified *force majeure* occurrences: for extension of the contract period and relief from delay penalties, in relation to other occurrences deemed to be outwith the contractor's control. Termination of the contract is possible in the event of serious specified default by the client. There are also ECGD and other forms of insurance available in appropriate cases.

Increasingly, there is an acceptance that it is most cost effective that risks should be borne by the party most able to effectively control their impact, and that to seek to impose on a contractor risks which it cannot influence is likely either to deter bidders or to increase bid prices by the inclusion of insurance costs or risk margins.

Nevertheless, there remain risks in overseas construction and the assessment and evaluation of these is an important part of the contractor's business.

The complexity of the risks may well render contractual risk analysis inappropriate; the size of project, the different areas of operation and infrequency of comparable projects necessitate an individual analysis of where risks may occur on each project.

5.3. Political and social

Government structure

In much overseas construction, the client is a government or governmental body and a contractor's relationship with the client or potential client is conditioned by government structure. Since the possibility of existence of a non-government or private sector is in turn dependent on government structure, its influence is virtually all-embracing. The changes in government structures in recent decades and their influence on the market for construction have been considerable.

In the colonial and immediately post colonial period much decision making rested in London through the agency of the Colonial Office or Crown Agents for the Colonies. Decisions were made on an unapologetically paternalistic, but largely incorruptible, basis. Former dependencies of other European countries had similar structures. Only isolated survivors of this system now remain.

In the early oil-boom years governments in the Middle East still largely followed the earlier tribal structure, and local rulers had virtually autocratic control (subject to the passive sanction of their supporters) of their territory and its rapidly escalating oil revenue.[54] This system enshrined free access to the ruler by the tribesmen and similar direct access was accorded to pioneering foreign businessmen. Such a system still has its apologists, contending that it enabled rapid decisions to be made and, in benevolently autocratic hands, displayed considerable achievements.

After colonialism there usually came democracy in one or other of its many forms, to continue or to be replaced in its turn by military coup. With multi-party democracy came party organisations and the recurring need to please some or all of the electorate. With single party democracy or with the oligarchy following a coup came an autocracy, akin to that of earlier times.

In many cases a construction project can play a part as an adjunct to building or enhancing the image of the regime. This can take the form of grandiose public buildings, palaces or monuments. It can also mean the construction of roads, schools, hospitals or mosques. In any of these cases there is scope for the equivalent of photo-opportunities at the start of work and at the formal opening. The timing of the project may have political significance and meeting a schedule, whether practical or not, may then become an overriding requirement of the contractor's construction programme.

A contractor wishing to work in a country has no alternative but to acknowledge the government structure, administration and bureaucracy. In many countries, where international contractors operate, there have been forecasts of the imminent overthrow of an existing regime and its replacement by one more congenial to an international contractor. Occasionally, a contractor has chosen to make a foothold in a country, in the anticipation of being established and so favourably placed when the anticipated change of government presented a more congenial regime. Threatened governments can survive for a long time and benefits from such anticipation can be long delayed.

Administration and bureaucracy
Under either autocratic or democratic systems there has been a continuous increase in bureaucracy, lengthening channels of communications and delays in the decision processes.

An understanding of the local ground rules is essential to a contractor, working or seeking to work in the country. A grasp of these rules can be expensive and painful to acquire. In some former UK colonies the bureaucracy seemed to reflect the earlier colonial structure which was based on a few relatively expensive expatriates at the top supported by a relatively inexpensively locally manned substructure. There are accompanying layers of control, each in turn checking on the layer below. At the other extreme were the few remaining autocratic rulers, who would deal directly and could be approached directly in case of subsequent difficulty.

The personnel within the bureaucracy are also significant. Where indigenous they are likely to reflect local educational standards and the status of professional administration in the local culture. Where administrators are recruited overseas their origin and the basis of their selection may reflect cost, or political, or religious affinity. Frequently such staff are lowly paid and there is a tacit acceptance that they will expect small inducements to promote timely actions.

The combination of an over elaborate bureaucratic structure and ill trained staff is an acknowledged recipe for inefficiency and delay. The sense of urgency of a contractor with a tight and enforceable programme to meet is sometimes at variance with the usual pace of local offices, and the overcoming of such difficulties can be tedious and time consuming. Where the due processing of a particular document is critical, contractors have arranged for a representative to accompany it on its path from desk to desk, as each clerk makes his necessary contribution to the process, to ensure that no avoidable delay occurs.

Language and legal system
In most developing countries there is a favoured foreign language, widely used commercially which is sometimes an official second language. In former colonies this is often the language of the earlier colonial power, with English, French, Spanish, Portuguese and Italian extensively used and understood in their respective areas, and with English enjoying a further extended field of use due to the commercial, military and political strength of the USA.

An important effect of this language bonding is in relation to further education, where the obvious convenience of a familiar language (combined with any residual familiarity of culture) is a powerful factor in the choice of destination for overseas study; although this factor is, in some cases, outweighed by factors of political or religious affinity, or more mundanely the availability of financial assistance.

The influence of European languages is overlapped, to a substantial degree, by that of legal systems. Often areas using the English language follow English law, while those using continental European languages follow systems akin to the French *Code Napoléon*, with the important exception of the increasing use by Islamic countries of Sharia law. The link of a European language to the legal system with the sheer practical problem of translating case law has the effect, in some instances, of entrenching the foreign language in the courts, while it is losing ground in commercial use. The increased general use of Cantonese in Hong Kong is an example of the phenomenon.

The contract documents may in externally aided projects specify international arbitration or the application of the law of the donor country.

Clearly, a known language and general familiarity with the legal system reduce the unknowns facing a contractor considering entry to a new territory. If the government officials share a common heritage by language or education then this is a further bonus. If they enjoyed their period of education and developed a favourable predisposition to the UK and to its standards and products, these factors can only help.

Social environment

Establishing a construction operation overseas involves the bringing together of two or more different cultures and many of the aspects of this interaction affect decisions made by the contractor.

At the core are its UK staff. There may be religious restrictions on alcohol or codes differing from those in the UK on the degree of segregation of men and women. Islamic standards of dress are a well-known irritant to women workers. Failure to conform to such requirements is likely to lead to friction which may harm working relationships; only the most extreme case will create international headlines.

Next comes the immigrant workforce, i.e. labour which is recruited from countries outside the location of the project. Again the likely compatibility of the nationalities and their religions need to be considered and may well influence the choice of area for recruitment.

There is also the question of social facilities and amenities, hospitals and medical care, schools and recreational facilities.

These, from the contractor's viewpoint, are some of the features of the social environment which need to be considered in forming a judgement as to how willing the staff and workforce would be to become part of the local community and how successful they would be in doing so; with this judgement reflected in the subsequent arrangements for performance of the project.

There is equally the other side of the relationship. In many cases a major construction project in a developing country is located in a relatively rural and unsophisticated area and is completed within a few years. During that period not only nationals employed on the project but also virtually everyone in the area is brought into contact with a very different way of life. To a degree this must foster ambitions and offer role models which may differ substantially from those traditional to the area. This is no longer universally considered as automatically a good thing in the onward march of progress.[55,56] The client may regard it as its responsibility to minimise such disturbance and, accordingly, require that the contractor's activities are as far as possible self contained. The contractor may reach a similar conclusion. More positively, the decision may be that more is to be gained than lost by the mingling of the two cultures.

Where facilities of the project are open to the local community, the personnel and their families need briefing and instruction on local customs and culture.

5.4. Operating conditions

Local construction industry

The local construction industry is a major element in the project environment and is potentially a resource, a joint stakeholder, a competitor or a combination of these.

Firms operating in the local industry can act as a subcontractor for particular elements of the project. This is a resource to the main contractor's advantage, for it provides a source of local manpower trained in basic construction skills.

The local construction industry is a joint stakeholder, particularly in government projects. One of the objectives of large projects in international settings is the development of the indigenous construction industry, which can then play a part in the development of the country. This objective can be explicit or implicit in its application. At one end of the spectrum there is no formal acknowledgement of this objective, but nevertheless local employees do acquire additional construction and management skills by working on the project. These enhanced capabilities are subsequently available to the local community. At the other extreme the development of local construction resources is explicitly recognised as a major objective. For example, design and performance specifications may be shaped to allow the maximum possible indigenous input; or the conditions of contract may require formal on-site or off-shore training of an expatriate contractor's local employees; or the tender conditions may be drafted to favour local bidders or bidders with local participation as partners or part owners.

Finally, local firms are competitors. When a local company has, or can assemble, the resources and expertise to undertake a major contract it may operate competitively and it may win a contract in open competition with expatriate contractors. However, it is more likely that local participation will have been recognised prior to the bidding stage. This could lead either to the exclusion of foreign bidders or to financial advantages to companies wholly or partly locally owned. If local contractors are to be preferred then design and specification which are advantageous to local resources, possibly linked to an extended period for construction, can be introduced in the design phase.[43,53] While the intent of these measures is to encourage local participation, their application has its own problems. Local part ownership may be a purely financial exercise, with no technical or training benefits when compared with a fully expatriate contractor. Labour intensive design, exclusion of imported materials and longer construction periods may increase overall costs and lose the opportunity of rapid development of skills.

The strength of the local construction industry varies enormously within the range of developing nations. It can be a headman assembling a small number of unskilled labourers or major companies capable of winning construction contracts inside and outside their own country. Such contractors are clearly in competition with developed nation contractors.

Competition

An over-simplification would, as noted earlier, show the post war UK overseas construction industry operating principally in three phases: firstly, from the immediate post war period to the late 1960s as in an extended and largely protected domestic market in the sterling area; secondly, from the late 1960s to the early 1980s as entrepreneurial contractors in the boom areas of the developing world and thirdly, from the early 1980s as financial investors in the Americas.[10,30,39] During these phases the pattern of international competition has also changed. In the first phase the main competition was with other UK contractors. Early parts of the second phase saw competition from mainland Europe and the US followed by Korea, Japan, China and Taiwan, all with considerable direction and support from their governments. Later in the second phase came Turkey, with India and Pakistan, seeking work on the back of large numbers of nationals operating as contract workers in the construction industry. Late entrants are likely to be Thailand and the Philippines.[10,11,30,34,35,47,57] This latter trend illustrates the rate of development of indigenous contractors.

Accordingly, competition for work in a developing country is likely to include international competition from any or all of the above countries. In addition, competition from the indigenous industry (where sufficiently developed) may be experienced. The local industry has considerable advantages; it will be familiar with local conditions and is likely to receive preference in the bidding or selection process which may seek to encourage local industry.

Further, a local contractor securing a contract by a low bid (against foreign competition) may look for underwriting by the client if its bid should prove too low.

In essence a UK contractor seeking work overseas must be prepared to accept that the playing field for bidding is unlikely to be level and that its marketing strategy should take account of this.

Employment market

A contractor on a major project in a developing country is

dependent on local labour for a part of its workforce.[58] This demand can have a substantial influence upon the local labour market. The degree of such influence is naturally dependent on the size of the project in relation to the local economy.

The existing capacity of the local labour market determines what proportion of its workforce the contract would wish to import. The degree of regulation of the labour market (formal or informal) determines the extent to which it would be able to import labour. The factors affecting the existing market are

o size of population
o state of development of the local construction industry
o skills acquired by local workers
o alternative sources of income
o the attractiveness of construction work in the local culture.

A contractor in some parts of the Middle East during the oil boom years, would employ a few well educated local staff on the administrative side of its management, with the whole of its technical and field supervision management being European expatriates.

A few Bedouin as drivers or watchmen would be employed but the rest of its workforce and administrative staff would be imported from the Indian subcontinent. Nationals did not seek technical skills, preferring commerce. In general, the indigenous population were so generously subsidised from oil revenues that they had no need to seek uncongenial employment. Driving expensive trucks over the desert at great speed was fun.

In many other areas there was a large population dependent on subsistence agriculture and any opportunity of paid work was welcomed.

The benefits of training a local workforce have been explained earlier but the downside of employing local labour is that the project provides temporary employment at relatively high wages which distort the local economy. After the project employees return to the local labour pool with no continuing demand for the largely specialised skills acquired.

In larger countries there are sometimes regional or tribal specialisations in skills and, accordingly, the workforce for a major project may include those from other regions in the country. This can inject an element of inter-regional rivalry or animosity. On one project in West Bengal in India a poster was seen: 'Punjabis, Madrassis, Nepalis and British go home'.

Materials, products and logistics

These are factors of the local environment of the project, which have immediate physical influence on the work to be performed by the contractor. In construction the primary raw materials are stone, aggregates and fill materials, some timber and, of course, water. The availability, suitability and location of these are crucial to the project. How the work is to be done and its cost will be influenced by the materials available.

A contractor is likely to choose to produce stone aggregates from quarried rock or gravel sources. He will need to locate, prove and secure technical and environmental approval of such sources and negotiate for their use. Sources and types of back-fill material may also have to be investigated. It may be that the economics of local material could call for modification to existing designs or specifications.

The availability of manufactured products is also important. For locally manufactured products the criterium is quality, which the proviso that modification to design or specification may be justified to utilise a local product which would not otherwise be acceptable. Other factors when reviewing local products are

o cost of transport   o quality of product
o duties payable   o reliability of supply.

The criteria for imported materials are

o quality of imported goods
o quantity and bulk
o costs
o import regulations
o currency exchange permits and duties
o the requirement to use local agents for particular manufacturers (some will provide a useful service, others will seek to exploit a monopoly position).

The importance of logistics can hardly be overstressed: the capacity of ports, roads, railways; the possible use of internal airborne or waterborne traffic; the possible need to construct new access to the working area will all need to be considered. In extreme circumstances, the constraints of the project programme may demand expensive solutions. In one instance, in a project 1000 kilometres from the nearest available roadhead, cement and all other supplies for a 4000 metre concrete runway were delivered by a combination of truck convoys over grader maintained desert track and chartered air transport. A project duration of ten months demanded such solutions.

Climate

Climate and associated disease was the cliche of overseas construction, with the image of intrepid pioneers overcoming burning desert and impenetrable tropic jungle and swamp. In the folklore of one company it is said that in its earlier contracts in the late 19th century, its commissary, as a wise precaution, carried an inscribed gravestone for each expatriate, which was duly ceremonially broken at his farewell party if he survived the tour.

Something has been done since then to ameliorate conditions but climatic factors continue. Working in a large hole in the sand, a shade temperature of 120°F is a little academic; there is no shade. Similarly, a million cusecs of seasonal flood water encircling a river bed excavation still presents problems. More mundanely, climate affects operations indirectly through its effect on personnel (and their families where they accompany them). It influences decisions on night and day working and the utilisation of equipment as such items need lighting and air-conditioning. Other influences include seasonal rains and flooding which interfere with operations, particularly of earthworks and require protection and diversion measures. Dust and sand affect the operation of equipment requiring special provisions and maintenance measures. Heat and cold restrict or require special measures in such operations as the mix design and placing of asphalt and concrete. Extreme heat critically influences the possible working conditions and life expectation of tyres for equipment.

Both individuals and operations have increasingly effective protection against the effects of climate but it remains a significant element in the construction environment.

Natural environment

In more recent times, the effect of the proposed works on the natural environment are a major factor in concept design and decision to proceed. This may be particularly so where international funding is involved. In some cases the conflict between environmental and human needs are not resolved to the satisfaction of all parties and continuing opposition to the concept of the works may interfere with construction.

The processes of construction will also have their impact upon the environment. The opening of quarries, borrow pits, access roads and temporary works areas, with associated erosion effects, change the natural landscape. The winning of raw timber where required, the pollution of waterways by discharges and in sensitive areas noise and dust pollution are critical issues. This impact must be contained within prescribed limits and the measures necessary to achieve this need incorporating into the project cost. Such measures as landscaping, lake formation, replanting and forestation, either in design or as a component of construction method, can reduce harmful effects and produce some offsetting benefit. Attitude of mind has a significant effect on the eventual balance between harm and benefit.

Part II

Making the pitch

In essence then, senior management determine aims, i.e., what the organisation seeks to be and what it seeks to do. The ways and means of achieving these aims will be the responsibility of project management working within the framework of a mandate. Periodically, senior management monitors the performance of this mandate. The mandate can be issued

o formally or informally
o in its entirety or in instalments
o openly or selectively.

It must take some account of commercial confidentiality.

Formally or informally
Some firms have induction manuals, issued to staff on appointment, or even shown to prospective staff before appointment. At their most complete these attempt to set out the culture of the company and its aims and the intended psychological contract between the company and its employees. At the other extreme a company believes that these matters are better unwritten, that the nature of the company is sufficiently made known by its reputation in the industry, and that employees best absorb the mores of the organisation by osmosis from working within it. Within most organisations there are members inclining more or less to one or other of these poles.

Entirety or instalments

An organisation's plans are short, medium and long term; self-evidently, the more remote, the less precise. Medium and long term plans are, inescapably, conditional on the degree of success or otherwise of the performance of short term planning. In the example of a company deciding to consider work overseas, there are a chain of decisions each dependent on the result of implementing the preceding decision. Typically the following sequence can be seen:

- o to carry out a desk study
- o to mount an assessment visit to establish a local office, agent or connection
- o to proceed with a specific tender or proposal.

Some companies avow a need to know policy and tell each individual as little as possible as late as possible. Others disseminate information fairly generally when it becomes firm but regard more distant possibilities, which may not come to fruition, as potentially unsettling for the general body of employees and, accordingly, better restricted to those who need them and are better able to evaluate them.

Openly or selectively

In an ideal world, all those who would wish to be considered as stakeholders are equally acknowledged as such, and the aims adopted by the company fully accommodate all the individual stakeholder's aims. In a nearly perfect world, most of those wishing to be stakeholders are acknowledged and most individual aims accommodated; and those unacknowledged or unaccommodated will stay aboard and perform loyally or disembark and depart doing no harm. Sadly, managements often find themselves wishing or needing to retain the services or goodwill of those they cannot fully acknowledge or accommodate and seek to fudge or blur announcements of decisions or policies in order to do so.

Commercial confidentiality

Few organisations wish to have their aims and intentions, even when entirely blameless, fully known and perhaps pre-empted by their competitors. Ready copying and transmission, coupled with varying concepts of loyalty and whistle blowing, make it moderately difficult to control absolutely the circulation of anything, once written.

The path through these conditions clearly needs to be chosen with care and the choice made inevitably reflects circumstances, the nature and culture of the organisation and the character of its management. There is no simple dictum that absolute openness or absolute secrecy is the best or even the most profitable course in all cases.

Subject to these considerations a mandate evolves. Usually, this is iterated and is subject to development as the project emerges.

In direct relation to overseas construction the mandate applies particularly to the decision to consider overseas work, the market evaluation and marketing effort to secure such work, the terms of acceptance of work, its performance and the securing of consequent remuneration or other benefit. Initially this work will focus upon marketing and subsequently project planning.

6

Marketing international construction

6.1. Operation

International contracting organisations are largely structured in a similar way to any other large construction firm. The chief executive leads a team of functional specialists which, typically, may be arranged as shown in Fig. 12. The structure classically sets out the lines of command, reporting and responsibility, and individuals are assigned or recruited to each designated role. However, it is unusual to find such rigidity in overseas construction. More typically, the structure is organic, there are relationships between individuals, some arising from overlapping of their functions, some from previous association on overseas projects and some merely from personal compatibility. These relationships, if properly managed, should complement and strengthen rather than detract from the formal organisation structure.

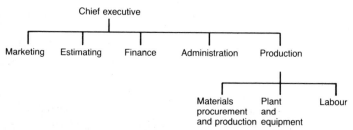

Fig. 12. The typical specialist team

Briefly, functions are designed to use to maximum advantage the particular abilities of the individuals who are the company's major asset and the organisation chart should aim to approximately record these rather than constrain them.

Where the overseas construction organisation is not an autonomous company but a subsidiary or division of a larger group, much of the foregoing can still apply. The overseas operation is usually separate, with a degree of conditional autonomy and may well have its own subsidiary company board or divisional board. The authority of such board is not absolute, and it may well include one or more non-executive nominees of the parent group. However, in most cases it cherishes such autonomy as it has and, as noted earlier, it is usually the case that the more successful its operations, the more its autonomy is respected. Subject to these reservations on authority, it and the chief executive can generally conduct themselves as an independent organisation.

In practice, the boundaries of departments are flexible. For example, when a specific marketing exercise is in hand an informal team will be formed combining individuals from as many departments as necessary.

6.2. Marketing strategy

Strategy and philosophy

The relationship between the marketing activity and a project is shown in Fig. 13. The reason for many construction companies operating in international markets is that margins are seen to be more generous than those at home. Consideration of the strategy and philosophy of marketing concentrates on aspects of work quality and client satisfaction;[12,32,34,39,47,58–64] although doing these profitably is a no less important element to most contractors.

The emphasis is on identification with the client so that its real needs, which may sometimes differ from the issued documents, are appreciated and efforts can be directed to the satisfaction of these needs. A commitment by the contractor to the client must be developed. It is noted that performance of a project after completion may ultimately be recognised as more important than possible overrun on time or cost, and that

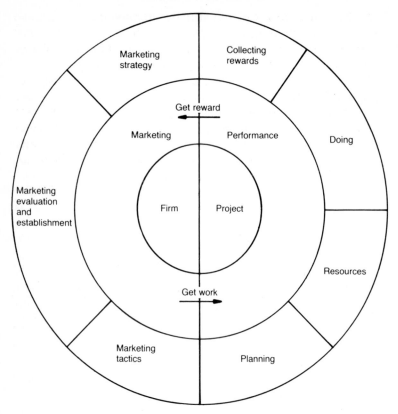

Fig. 13. Relationship between the marketing activity and the project

sensitivity to cultural differences is important both in marketing and in performance. To further this aim, a contractor should concentrate on what it can do best; it will generally be inclined to work within its capabilities and prefer to do work in which it has some edge in expertise or performance over likely competitors. It may be willing to extend its capabilities by recruitment, subcontract or joint venture if necessary.

The contractor will generally have a range of acceptable contract value, particularly in a new area. The maximum value is fixed by the contractor's ability to finance, or within this by its desire to avoid undue concentration of risk: the minimum, by the need to recover initial setting up costs.

In the early 1980s one contractor worked on the basis that a contract in isolation in a new area needed to be at least £30 million in value (about £60 million in 1994 values) to recover setting up costs and withdrawal on completion. Smaller contracts would, however, be sought where there was a prospect of continuing work where its assets could be used effectively.

There is much common ground in these observations, and this is likely to be evidenced in the marketing strategy developed by the contractor as a means to fulfilling the given mandate and contributing to the corporate aims. There are simple pointers

- a contractor is likely, where a choice exists, to prefer negotiated to tendered work
- any form of marketing is costly in money and effort
- a contractor will seek to apply its marketing effort in areas where it seems most likely to be cost effective, and seek to determine this by searches in potentially fruitful markets
- a contractor is also likely to apportion its marketing effort between tendered and other work to spread risk and optimise contracts awarded against the costs of marketing. In the main, negotiated contracts will carry a higher margin but will require greater expenditure on marketing.

Having determined an overall marketing strategy on such basis, a contractor will still seek to accommodate, within such strategy, *ad hoc* opportunities which appear favourable.

Market search
The first relatively passive means of finding a lead to a market is to subscribe to the appropriate publications and scrutinise the invitations to tender. Selection of those which seem compatible with the organisation's capabilities will necessitate a judgement on the advantages or disadvantages of working in the location. Sending a tender party will be the next step. The obvious disadvantage of this approach is that the period between tender invitation and required submission is never as long as a contractor would wish. A contractor has difficulty assessing the project, and collecting and evaluating the necessary information on the country within the tender period. It is sometimes possible to extend this period by advance information on the coming issue of an invitation to tender before its

actual publication. Some commercial organisations such as oil companies prepare, through their resident representatives overseas, lists of future tenders of which advance notice is available and are prepared to provide these to their customers. Some professional companies and some embassies or High Commission offices may be willing to provide similar advance information if approached.

The alternative is to consider potential work areas first without imposed time constraints; and specific work opportunities later, if the area appears encouraging. Initial leads to specific areas can come from in-house knowledge of members of the company or from a network of contacts in the construction environment. These contacts could be professional consultants, specialist subcontractors or equipment suppliers, etc. Such firms are likely to provide complementary rather than competing services. More formal information may be received from government or industry bodies. The next stage is likely to be a desk study. One approach is to gather, for as wide a range of countries as possible, a range of statistical indicators and to tabulate comparable information for the country or area under consideration. This enables the contractor to get a feel for the meaning of these indicators and compare them with those for areas with which it is familiar. Such a tabulation may sometimes of itself highlight areas of possible interest, without other initial lead.

Statistical indicators tabulated may well include

- area
- population
- gross national product
- per capita income
- main export products
- debt and credit rating
- membership of economic groupings such as OPEC, the Organization of South East Asian Nations (OSEAN), and the American Pacific Organization for Economic Cooperation (APEC)
- indigenous contracting industry
- state of infrastructure
- provision of schools, hospitals, etc.
- current construction activity, etc.

Some of this information can be acquired from the country's representative office in the UK, or from United Nations or similar publications. Sometimes a useful contribution to the desk study can be made by hearsay information from the management's ongoing networking. The desk study may appear tedious and time consuming. It is much less costly than the later stages of evaluation and may avoid incurring abortive costs later in the process.

Unsolicited approaches

By introductions or by direct approaches, most contractors are offered leads to potential projects or to areas in which it would be to their advantage to seek work. The individual acting as a middleman may be a national of the country concerned, an expatriate resident or an expatriate itinerant through various countries of the region. The middleman will usually offer introductions and guidance on the appropriate proposal to be made. Almost always this person will seek some payment either as a retainer or on results, or both, and it is not unusual for them to explain that where any substantial payments are sought, these are not wholly for their retention, but include disbursements which are unavoidable if the proposal is to bear fruit.

Most contractors turn down most such approaches. Some are followed up at some cost. Of these, some lead directly or indirectly to work in the recommended area. No reliable rule book has been established to determine which approach is worth following, the judgement of this is an important marketing skill and, as many such, a combination of instinct and experience.

6.3. Market evaluation and establishment

Evaluation

This involves physically assessing the area under consideration. If this visit follows an approach to the company by an entrepreneur it is likely that this person will wish to take the lead in the arrangements for the visit. From his (and in most cases, although no longer invariably, it is a he) viewpoint this may help to enhance his credibility with local contacts by being seen to deliver 'his' contractor. It may also help to maintain the contractor's dependency on the entrepreneur by ensuring that contacts established during the visit also involve the entrepreneur.

The contractor, on the other hand, will wish to obtain an independent view and to this end is likely to establish a network of contacts to corroborate or challenge the evidence being presented. Leads, to this end, may be found through the UK Embassy or High Commission, banks, oil companies, or other commercial or professional organisations established in the area.

The balance between the two has some delicacy and face enters the equation. The entrepreneur may well insist that the contractor should demonstrate trust and good faith by leaving matters entirely to him, the contractor may wish to keep open its options without giving offence. Each will make an assessment of the relative strengths of their positions.

If the contractor has selected the area for evaluation without the involvement of a local entrepreneur, then it is likely that the arrangements for the visit will have to be made through contacts independent of a local entrepreneur. To be worthwhile the visit party must include, or be led by, a member of the company of sufficient weight and position to command reception and acknowledgement in the area being visited and to ensure that their reports and conclusions are likely to be accepted and acted upon. Such visits are expensive; time spent waiting in hotels is largely unproductive. Accordingly, as much as possible should be done to arrange the first level of contacts before leaving, while retaining flexibility on arrangements thereafter. The purpose of the visit is to assess the prospect of a marketing exercise contributing to opening up of profitable and well executed work. This means assessing the total environment of a proposed project and, in particular, the opportunities to secure work by submission and acceptance of proposals, or by invited tender at a level of pricing sufficient to allow due performance and profit.

At one level, this involves putting flesh on the bones of the preceding desk study, verifying the procedures for award of contracts and subsequent payment, and broadly assessing potential local contributions to performance. At the next level, it involves an assessment of individuals and personalities including the entrepreneur and client involved. An assessment of the level of competition that a contractor may face will also need to be made.

It can be seen that to include such an investigation as simply a part of a tender visit, between award and submission, is not easy. The routines of a tender visit are briefly considered later but suffice it to say that the amount of information to be gathered is large when compared to the time available. If the area and project assessments are undertaken concurrently and the area assessment is negative then the other inputs to tendering are abortive.

Getting started

If the assessment on the ground leads to a positive decision, the next step is either to proceed directly with the current tender, or towards a proposal for a specific project. If the general environment is favourable but no appropriate project is imminent, then it may be best to establish a presence in the area with the intention of identifying an appropriate project on which to proceed in the future. During the evaluation process a company's name becomes, to a degree, identified with the person leading the evaluation team and there is generally acknowledged to be a significant advantage in familiarity and continuity. If the individual is well accepted this asset should be maintained and the same face should continue to be seen representing the company in further visits during the getting started period, and he should also seek to maintain contacts by any other means available.

Local representatives

At this stage, it is usually necessary to consider the appointment of a local agent. This might be the entrepreneur whose approach led the company into the area, or a national introduced by him or selected during the assessment visit. The role of a local agent was mentioned earlier as a potential stakeholder and this role is shaped by the customs and organisation of the country and its decision making process. This may range from a ruler with an informal semi-public council to an elaborate and politicised bureaucracy.

The choice of agent is vital; if the agent is inadequate or is unacceptable in critical quarters much potentially useful effort can be wasted. Once appointed an agent is difficult to change, doing so usually involves resentment and letting loose an active illwisher in the area, or additional cost in compensation to avoid this. It may seem ironic that an agent replaced, because he is insufficiently powerful to do the contractor good, may still be strong enough to do harm.

If an agent is not introduced by the entrepreneur, the contractor will probably wish to seek one, and may be guided in this by the contacts established during the assessment visit. Almost inescapably many more will offer their services. The separation of the wheat from the chaff in these potential agents is a skill; in comparison water divining is childishly simple and logical. Most of those offering their services will present themselves as able to provide influence as well as contacts. One of the first lessons to learn is that the two do not necessarily go together. It is sometimes a matter of simple courtesy in the local culture to receive a visitor graciously or even warmly. A contact may be impressively efficient in arranging introductions and meetings, and still give assurances of influence which are absolutely without foundation.

Influence is the magic ingredient. Its basis depends on the custom and culture of the country of operation. Most contacts offer it, some sponsors and some partners can deliver.

Local marketing

A sponsor is a local personality who agrees to sponsor the incoming contractor. At times and in some places in the Middle East, official decrees dictated that no foreign contractor could operate without a registered local sponsor. The sponsor was often far too eminent to perform the duties of an agent, although he might assist by nominating one, but the contractor hoped that he would exert influence. The effectiveness of such influence, against a more favourable competing proposal, could seldom be reliably predicted.

Occasionally, as noted earlier, a local merchant would provide funds to become a financial partner, or a local contractor would contribute construction capability to become a working partner. To encourage this process, tender regulations sometimes prescribed a minimum local percentage holding in a company wishing to tender, either as a condition of acceptance, or to qualify for a preference adjustment in adjudication of tender prices. Sometimes to meet such prescription, a local sleeping partner would be funded and indemnified against loss.

The alternative means of establishing a local presence is to install a member of the company management as local representative, with a small office. The notional advantage of this is that it reduces the degree of reliance on a local agent and, in favourable circumstances, makes it possible to delay appointment of a local agent, until this can be done on the basis of better knowledge. Such an establishment costs money and the likelihood of its being effective depends not only on the individual, but also on whether the local culture is receptive to the required networking by a newly arrived foreigner. Otherwise it may achieve little more than to serve as a postbox for possible tender invitations.

Either way, the appointment of an agent or the establishment of an office is seen as a commitment to activity and the local agent or expatriate representative is likely to see their position as dependent on the quantum of such activity. They are likely to be influenced by this factor and press for the pursuance of tenders or other opportunities, incurring expenditure which head office may not consider to be cost effective.

The establishment of a local marketing presence and the means of doing so are important decisions. Most of the alternative means have had their successes and not surprisingly there is an element of chicken and egg. The most appropriate arrangement for a local establishment is best made on the basis of detailed understanding of the area, its customs, procedures and personalities. The development of such understanding is a major purpose of setting up the local establishment. The correct choice for each circumstance requires experience, commercial judgement, research and advice and, as in so many other aspects, is helped by good luck.

6.4. Marketing tactics

Proposals and product tailoring

A brief reference was made earlier, while considering the international environment, to possible disadvantages of the traditional system of open competitive tender and the development of alternative contractual arrangements. There are many variants, all receiving wide consideration, and for which reasoned cases can be made.[12,17,35,39,47,65-72]

Such alternatives include

o turnkey	o target estimate
o design and construct	o cost-plus.

Recently, standard conditions of contract documents have been designed to cover such alternatives.

Most contractors would admit to preferring to negotiate for work rather than to tender. This does not necessarily show a desire or intention to exploit a captive customer, but a contractor would usually acknowledge that the fear of such possible exploitation does exist in the mind of some potential clients.

The advantage of negotiation, from a contractor's viewpoint, is that the risk element of being bound to uneconomic tender is largely avoided, as is the cumulative cost of unsuccessful tenders (although proposals also involve costs which can equally be abortive) while agreed margins in negotiation may well exceed the margins included in a tender in highly competitive conditions.

The advantages of negotiation which a contractor would seek to commend to a potential client include

● the ability to choose a contractor on suitability and record
● the delivery of the fast track approach by

    o eliminating tender periods
    o concurrent design and construction

● the introduction of value engineering by

    o involving the contractor in design and planning
    o incorporating expertise and knowledge of the resources of the area.

Reasonably, it can be contended that the major cost decisions in any project are necessarily made before completion of design and that, accordingly; this is the period in which major savings are most probable. The traditional tender system concentrates its control of costs in the period after completion of design, and the economies in time and money from fast track and value engineering can more than offset any believed saving on contractors' margins from competitive tendering.

In pursuing the possibility of non-tendered work the contractor will approach potential clients to consider their possible requirements. It may then discover that the potential client has a number of potential projects, all at a fairly advanced stage of formulation and design, but is unable to proceed further for lack of funding. In many areas this is the legacy of earlier international funding of feasibility studies and failure to complement this by construction funding. In other areas the contractor may readily identify obvious needs for development, but find that the potential client has only the barest ideas towards progressing these, or may even be able to suggest valid development projects which the client has not previously considered or appreciated.

The possibility of pursuing such an approach depends on a high degree of confidence between the contractor and potential client. The confidence is based upon the quality of

o the contractor's record
o the contractor's access to the client
o the local agent
o the head office marketing team.

Where such confidence is established and a contractor seeks to present a proposal involving major construction works, that contractor must seek to establish with the potential client what 'its' requirements and priorities are and then design a formal proposal to accommodate these as fully as possible.

The contractor may reach the conclusion during this initial stage that it cannot, or should not, submit the intended proposal. There are a number of possible good reasons for this. Early study may show the project to be unsound for physical reasons, geological or climatic factors, or on economic grounds in that assessment of foreseen costs and benefits shows it to be unviable, or simply because the contractor is unable to include a necessary element of funding in its proposal. It is also possible that such early study may reveal that the client's aims are better achieved by alternative means which do not require construction and so offer no role or involvement for the contractor. There can be no doubt that the contractor must then advise the client accordingly. This is a clear requirement of the confidence established between the contractor and client. It is also basic commercial prudence; the contractor's reputation for trustworthiness is a major marketing asset, particularly in negotiated work.

Where the contractor is satisfied that it can and should proceed, the formal proposal may comprise a virtual shopping list, intended to allow the client to deal with the contractor as a single entity, or one-stop, for as much as it wishes.

Alternatively, earlier discussion and assessment of the project may establish that the client's organisation has considerable capability which needs only to be complemented by specific specialist services. In such a case the UK contractor may suspend its main contracting role and offer only specialist services, perhaps construction management and/or equipment procurement.

Subject to this proviso, the shopping list could include

o concept design
o feasibility study
o project definition
o land acquisition
o finance
o detailed design

o supervision
o construction and
   construction management
o equipment procurement
o project commissioning
o operation and training.

The contractor would then assemble a group to include such design consultants, bankers, suppliers and specialist subcontractors as the project required.

The conditions of contract within the formal proposal could then be formulated to place each element of risk with the party who could most effectively control such risk. They should also seek to allay any residual fears the client may have of possible exploitation by introducing one or more review stages. These would be timed to precede further major financial commitment and, at each such stage, the contractor would present to the client's officers or independent advisers the latest developed information on foreseen costs, returns and viability. The client would have the option, in the light of such information, to terminate the contract on payment of the contractor's costs incurred and a predetermined stage fee.

The proposal itself needs to be concise, understandable and reasonably attractive and impressive in appearance. Internal company desktop publishing capacity usually allows this; although with additional expenditure a computer/video presentation, more or less elaborate or futuristic, can be added. A contractor will often prefer the proposal document to include a form of preliminary acceptance, intended to be signed by the client at the end of the presentation visit so that momentum towards the implementation of the project is maintained. The team presenting the proposal is important and its make up must depend on the progress already made by the company towards getting started in the area. Its members need to exude

- familiarity—a face the client identifies with the company
- authority—someone able to agree changes if necessary
- command—someone who has command of the technical contents of the proposal.

This virtually dictates that the most senior member of the company already known in the area and the local agent, if appointed, should be part of the team, which should arrive with the intention of reaching agreement before leaving and be prepared to stay as long as necessary to do so.

Invited competitive tenders
In the traditional process a client, through a professional consultant or in-house expert, produces design and contract documents and invites tenders, usually with a fairly short tender period. Quite often the invitation states that only conforming tenders will be considered, making it very difficult for a contractor to make, or to benefit from, any contribution to value engineering.

Contractors will respond to tender invitations in conventional ways and most contractors have a tender questionnaire or check list for use during the tender site visit to assist tender preparation. This questionnaire is designed to define the project environment as briefly considered in chapter 5. The location related items include

 o local political and administrative structure
 o taxes
 o exchange regulations
 o general commercial facilities
 o transport and communication facilities
 o available subcontract or workforce skills
 o terms of employment.

Taken at face value this location related information seeks to act as a shortened version of the area assessment considered earlier. If the information indicates unacceptable difficulties the contractor may decide against completing and submitting a tender. Occasionally, a tender visit team expends considerable effort in uncomfortable conditions assembling the project related information, only to find this happen.

The project related items include

- o main work quantities
- o nature and geology of site
- o access
- o climate and hydrology
- o need for, and availability of, natural quarry, borrow pit or other materials
- o locally manufactured or imported materials
- o the administration of the project contract, particularly the supervising and certifying and payment authorities.

Where the contractor already has a local establishment, the area related information should be available and should be continuously refined and updated. Where the contractor has general information on the project in advance of the issue of formal documents, some elements of both area and project information can be assembled. Such advance notice may be provided by the contractor's general intelligence in the area or it may be an uncovenanted benefit of the client's decision to advertise for prequalification before inviting tenders. Such an invitation to prequalify is designed, as noted earlier, to avoid an excessive number of tenders from bidders who may be unable to perform satisfactorily and whose participation may either distort the tender process or drive away more desirable bidders. The prequalification questionnaire usually requires particulars of the contractor's resources in personnel, in equipment and finance and its relevant experience. The terms of the questions asked must alert a contractor to the general nature, location and intended timing of the project. This enables information to be acquired. Subsequent invitations to tender are restricted to contractors selected from those satisfactorily completing the prequalification process.

Planning and estimating
Where contract documents are issued by the client, which is usually the case in invited tenders as opposed to contractors'

proposals, the contractor, generally, will wish to study the contract conditions at the early stage of preparing a tender and, if these seem unduly onerous, may decline to tender. Most issued documents derive from one or other of the current standard conditions documents with FIDIC, issued by the Fédération Internationale des Ingenieurs-Conseils, most used internationally. A study of the contract normally seeks to identify alterations or particular conditions, with sensitive aspects including

o provisions for client default
o on-demand bonds
o the professional autonomy of the engineer
o applicable law or arbitration
o contract advances and repayments.

These provisions must be judged alongside any knowledge or experience the contractor may have of the client's dealings on previous contracts and in parallel with consideration of the nature of work and total value of the project.

Normally the site tender visit, the study of documents and the planning and estimating are all put in hand concurrently. A tender team is assembled consisting of selected available members of the estimating and project co-ordination branches. The tender visit party consists of members of this team, often with co-opted assistance from any suitable company staff resident in and familiar with the project area. The balance of the team proceed with document study, planning and estimating, incorporating in this such interim information as the visit party can transmit. The full team reassembles on return of the visit party with the balance of their information.

In essence, the estimating team for a major construction project attempt to plan the construction and then to assess the costs of the operations involved under appropriate cost heads. Mercifully, the 80/20 law still applies (20% of the work items constitute 80% of the total cost) and their efforts can be concentrated on major cost items, with minor items included from previous knowledge or record.

The appropriate cost heads for such an estimate are usually

• labour: inclusive costs of the project workforce
• materials: local and imported, including any permanent installed equipment

- construction plant operation: principally spares, tyres, fuels and consumables
- plant ownership: the capital cost of the construction plant over the period of the project
- local on-costs: essentially, everything but labour, materials and plant, and including accommodation, offices and workshops, expatriate supervisory staff and expatriate and local management and administrative staff
- subcontracts: local or offshore
- head office mark-up: including a recovery of head office overheads, costs of finance and allowances for risk and profit.

A tender plan and programme for performance is central to the exercise. It must meet the contract programme, subject to a policy decision to provide for any penalty costs of overrun; it must also allow for mobilisation periods, covering the necessary time to move equipment to the site, including any delivery delays on any essential new equipment and any peculiarities of ports or inland transport in the area. A key issue is often the installation and commissioning of quarrying and crushing equipment, concrete, asphalt and similar installations. Provision must also be made for any seasonal interruptions to progress arising from natural causes such as climate or floods, or from religious or other observances.

Experienced estimators contend that a sensible workmanlike plan is at this stage sufficient, that refinements of method may allow savings later, but that at tender stage they are unlikely to influence greatly the total price and that the time to pursue them is not available. There is no doubt that, from time to time, instances of inspiration in tender planning prove the exceptions to this rule. One such example is the case where a quarry was meant to be filled with excavated material and very little of the excavated material was to be carted off site. The estimating team inspected the site and formed the view that the quarry would not take all of the excavated material by a long way. Consequently, they priced the small amount of cart away material very advantageously. They were awarded the contract and were well pleased to negotiate a highly profitable rate for the additional carting away of the excavated spoil.

Within the plan and programme, manpower requirement is determined on the assessment of local skills and productivity, and any consequent need to supplement these by the importation of necessary skills. Similarly, plant requirement is determined in relation to assessed outputs, related to locally acceptable working shifts, and any diminution of performance due perhaps to temperature or to skill of available operators. This requirement is then adjusted to comprise equipment available within the company or requiring to be purchased with preliminary prices obtained. The costs of the operation are assessed from company experience, adjusted for local costs related to transport or local purchase and local factors, such as greater wear and tear on tyres in high temperatures or on poor roads, digger or crusher teeth in abrasive material and engine filters in dusty, sandy conditions.

Costs of ownership are, at this stage, based on standard depreciation, subject to any subsequent adjustment during settlement, with transport costs assessed separately.

Permanently installed equipment and permanent and temporary works materials are scheduled and, as for construction equipment, temporary or check prices obtained. The contractor wishes to obtain prices from suppliers which will be honoured if the tender is successful. It is conscious, however, that with the contract awarded it is in a stronger buying position, and may be able to negotiate more favourable prices from the chosen supplier or from alternative suppliers. There is, consequently, a degree of imprecision on the commitment of pre-tender supply quotations which sometimes occurs, similarly, in relation to pre-tender subcontract quotations. On site, on-cost items are similarly planned and building, staff and associated costs assessed. The dividing line between direct site costs and site on-costs, is necessarily imprecise and varies between companies, but is unimportant provided that the division is understood in settling the tender, and that provision is made under one head or other for all costs which will be incurred.

It can readily be seen that, for a major contract, a considerable number of factors and pieces of information need to be taken into account and evaluated. Since this has to be done under pressure of time there is clearly possibility for error. While most estimating departments have systems of cross checks designed to detect major errors, in which they profess complete confidence, it is also said that sometimes the lowest, and accordingly successful, price is the one containing the biggest error.

The procedures of estimating for negotiated work are basically similar, since the contractor and client both wish to know what the works will cost. There are, however, substantial differences, conditioned by the type of contract governing the negotiated works, which may be simple fixed lump sum, but is more likely to include arrangements for progressive revaluation, to take advantage of any progressive value engineering contributions and also to allow the client to consider cancellation of the contracts, where stage options to do so are provided. An overriding difference is that there is no comparable arbitrary time constraint requiring a final price for all items, so that interim revaluation matters which are not finalised can be treated on an on-account basis without detracting significantly from the overall reliability of the revaluation.

Tender settlement

Adjudication is usually by a committee. In this committee the tender team present the estimate to management for review and for development into the required tender or offer. The tender team usually comprises the chief estimator, supported by one or more of his team, either full time or simply when their detailed knowledge of the estimate assumptions or make-up are needed. The management group, similarly, comprises one or more directors and other heads of department in relation to the necessary performance by their departments if the tender succeeds and the contract is to be performed.

The size and formality of the adjudication committee reflects the culture and style of the company. At the one extreme, the chief estimator reports to the managing director who makes the decision, and others are called in as, and only as, their contributions are wanted. At the other extreme, all senior members of the tender team and all affected heads of department participate as of right and contribute to a discussion aimed at reaching a consensus. In either case the MD may adjourn proceedings and resolve critical issues either in silent contemplation or with the aid of an informal kitchen cabinet.

Commitment to, and ownership of, the tender submitted is vital for the senior managers. For it is they who will have to live with the consequences of the financial outcome of the project long after the tender has been completed.

The format of the presentation sheets has usually evolved within the company over the years, sometimes with an element of cross-fertilisation as estimators move from one company to another. Usually such sheets include an analysis make-up of labour, plant, materials and subcontracts; for each bill of quantities (BOQ) item and in total. The plant make-up sheet, similarly, analyses plant operation and ownership costs for each major operational section of the work and in total. Again, usually there is a settlement summary sheet summarising the estimate subtotals of the cost heads as for the estimate with adequate space for adjustments, risks or opportunities, prices and head office mark-up.

As an example, such an analysis reduced to percentages might produce Table 1 (the figures do not relate to any particular work). This type of analysis offers one more strand of information to the adjudication committee, allowing the weighted impact on total price of any adjustment to any one such element to be readily assessed. It also allows the contractor's position in comparison with a competitor, in relation to any one such element, to be assessed.

Table 1. Typical settlement summary sheet

	Site cost: %	Total price: %
Direct costs:		
Labour	11·0	9·8
Materials	29·0	25·9
Plant operation	27·0	24·1
Plant ownership	10·0	8·9
Subcontracts	10·0	8·9
Site on-costs:		
Expatriates	5·0	4·5
Other costs	8·0	7·1
Total site cost	100·0	89·2
Apportioned head office costs	3·0	2·7
Other costs through head office	4·0	3·6
Allowed profit	5·0	4·5
Total selling price	112·0	100·0

Factors which may come into such consideration could include

- labour: a competing bidder may have a different source of imported labour, perhaps from the bidder's own country. Such a source may be state controlled or subsidised. UK expatriates are no longer unduly expensive in comparison to western European or US companies, but they are likely to be much more costly in salaries and support costs than the staff of a developing nation bidder. They may nevertheless be at least, equally cost effective.
- materials: again a competitor may have access to a subsidised source. The contractor may be able to make an adjustment, based on being able to obtain overall more favourable rates when purchasing, than when enquiring for a tender. The amount, if any, is a matter of experience and judgement.
- plant operation: a competitor could have subsidies on spares. Otherwise, this element is a matter of wise plant selection and management of plant availability and productivity.
- plant ownership: there is some room for flexibility in company policy on depreciation. Competitors may have equal or more room.
- subcontracts: possibly some scope for rate bargaining after award.
- head office costs: long term these can only be recovered from projects; the amount of recovery from the project in question is subject to policy decision.
- other site costs: these include non-UK staff, offices and workshops.
- other costs through head office: these include finance, insurance and any allowances for exceptional risk. The costs are real but some competitors may neglect to include them and some, through state support, may escape them.

All these factors will be considered by the committee. An experienced estimator could predict, for a particular project, the order of total project value and approximate percentages as the tabulation above; this prediction could be done reasonably reliably within a day or two of receiving documents and drawings, and this early forecast may be a useful factor, concurrent with the document scrutiny, in deciding whether the contractor should or should not bid.

Where a contractor decides against preparing and submitting a competitive bid, there is a possibility that it may wish to maintain appearances by being seen to bid reasonably, and may have the opportunity of submitting a cover bid at a price fed to it by a friendly competitor just sufficiently in excess of the competitor's own bid. This seems to be fairly unusual in international bidding, due perhaps to a lack of complete trust and the consequent danger of adjustments by either party. The alternative form of cover occurs where a contractor, to take out competition, offers another an inducement if it will submit a price just sufficiently above that of the initiator, who thus secures the award. These black arts are not recommended and certainly are counter to the policies and procedures advocated by any of the international aid agencies and organisations such as the EU.

Whatever the form or structure of the committee, the estimating team present their estimate and explain the assumptions, reasoning and build-up of the items which they consider important, or which other members of the committee raise. In a more informal committee there is full and frank discussion of particular items. This may reflect individuals' particular experience or simply a difference in viewpoint between the estimator and another department. Any changes agreed to the estimate are noted as potential adjustments. The relatively recent application of computers to this type of estimating allows the impact of a number of such possible changes to be considered on a 'what if' basis before final decision. This, in effect, represents the first stage of settlement.

The second stage is a review of possible policy adjustments under risks or opportunities. These comprise items, noted by the estimating team or raised by others, which are less black and white than the preceding adjustments. They could include a policy decision on the charging to the project of depreciation on construction equipment; the risks and financial cost of irrecoverable time overrun; the possibility of savings on renegotiation of purchase or subcontract prices; savings if a new technique should prove effective, or any other comparable possibilities. The assessed financial cost or saving for each item, if it should occur, is noted in full but not at this stage treated as an adjustment.

Finally, mark-up additions are considered, these include any finance costs—calculated on a cash flow assessment based on final offer price—apportionment of head office overheads and provision for any on-scheduled costs and for company profit. Essentially, the most likely combined impact of risk and opportunity items is to be evaluated. This leads to a commercial judgement on the price included for risk; here some element of flexibility of policy is possible, with respect to depreciation, recovery of head office overhead and profit provision.

This judgement involves a feel for the local market, as much knowledge as possible of the intentions of competing bidders and the results of recent tenders. It will be substantially influenced by the contractor's need for work at the time and any special importance of the particular project to the contractor's local interests. The relatively small number of major projects in any one overseas area at one time normally precludes any benefit being gained from a statistical analysis of competitors' bids.

The conclusion of this process is a final offer price and single figure which is given to the chief estimator to allow the various mark-up elements to be distributed over the BOQ items for the tender submission.

In this distribution the estimator may, to a degree, seek to load more heavily items which seem certain to occur and quantities which seem likely to increase; and also those items, particularly preliminaries, which will be payable early in the contract period and so assist cash flow.

The tender adjudicators will in their turn, during scrutiny of the tender, seek to ensure that this has not been done to such a degree as to be harmful to the client's interest.

Contract negotiation and award

In an invited tender, the offer is in theory fully compliant and unconditional and award is to be expected to the lowest bidder at the bid price. The actuality is rarely quite so clear cut.

It is not unusual for a contractor to discover, usually after award, something in the documentation of his offer which can be construed as a condition and a possible basis for extra payment. If this is seen during scrutiny of bids by the client or its engineer, the contractor may be required to withdraw the condition, and may sometimes be granted an adjustment to tender price on this account. On disclosure of bid prices, if the lowest three or four bids are reasonably closely spaced, there may be a mild Dutch auction, initiated by the client or by the contending bidders jockeying for position.

Alternatively, where the lowest bid is far below the other contenders, the low bidder may discover or fear a mistake and may seek to adjust matters. It can forfeit its bid bond and withdraw; it may seek to withdraw without forfeiture, and this may be conceded. It may seek to retain the award, but to increase the price to something closer to the opposition, or it may choose to soldier on, with award at the bid price, in anticipation of being able to recover later.

There is the further hurdle that the client may not proceed with the contract. This may be due to changes in local, political or other conditions, or because bid prices were substantially above expectations and the financial provisions made, or because anticipated funding failed to materialise.

The usual view is that the low bidder should not count its chickens, and that the near contenders should not abandon hope. Accordingly, each of them is likely to continue representations and lobbying, and it is at this stage that established relationships and the influence of the local agent or connections are mobilised and put to the test.

In a proposal or offer for negotiation, the contractor has developed its marketing establishment and connections. The contractor has sought to understand the needs of the potential client and to reach an accord with the client's representatives.

The contractor prepares a proposal, which is viable and meets the client's needs and which the contractor believes is of mutual benefit to the client and the contractor. This proposal, depending on circumstances, may be a firm offer of defined work for quantified payment; it may be a shopping list of a range of services needed to implement the project from which the client, hopefully in co-operative interaction with the contractor, can select those it needs. The proposal may offer stages for review and possible cancellation as the project develops.

The contractor now wishes the project to proceed to completion with a minimum of further delay. This does not always, or inevitably, happen. There are major examples of successful project creation.[66,73] There are undoubtedly many more where well considered proposals failed to come to fruition and well presented documents lie in contractors' archives or line the walls of potential clients' offices.

Potential reasons for failure of a proposal can include

- the resurfacing of a residual fear that negotiation allows the exploitation of a captive customer
- discord arising between contractor and client, as to the relative benefits each is to derive from the project
- the client proving unable to provide the required input to the project
- the contractor proving unable to provide the required input to the project
- changing circumstances in the area or in the client's responsibilities or structure removing the wish to proceed
- one of the review stages provided demonstrating that the project fails to meet the client's needs
- one of the review stages provided demonstrating that the client's needs can better be met by some means other than the proposal and without the proposed construction.

If a project is abandoned as a result of a review this is a regrettable occurrence for the contractor but little can be done since withdrawal was specifically provided in the documents requesting the proposal.

The risk of the other causes can be reduced by the degree of care in preparation of the proposal; in the groundwork of the preliminaries in establishing a mutual appreciation of the client's needs. The presentation and explanation of the proposal tabled will be influential. The strength of established relationships, the quality of the local agent, and the competence and salesmanship of the presenting team are all important in achieving a successful negotiation.

Part III

'Doing the necessary'

This section addresses the issues surrounding the mobilisation of resources necessary for a contractor to build an international construction project. It focuses upon the project planning and project management with the management of key resources such as labour, materials, plant and equipment.

These resources have, of course, to be managed within a safety and quality framework and these matters are discussed in the work on project management.

7

Project planning

This chapter outlines the activities necessary for the performance of major construction work in an overseas territory following award of a contract after one or other of the processes considered in Part II. This award is, hopefully, on terms and at a price which the contractor considers will, subject to any provisions for adjustment of price in the terms, cover the costs of performance of the contract.

International projects, like any other, have to balance the objectives of time, cost and quality and these are usually considered as mutually conflicting. It has been said that there is 'good', 'quick' and 'cheap'; a client can have any two. The practical aim is sufficing in all three rather than seeking to optimise one, although particular circumstances may dictate priorities such that, for one of the three elements, sufficing is close to optimising.

To illustrate the principles of performing a project, a sequence of actions is described in the following section. The project is let under the traditional design, tender and build method. This part of the book is broken down into the planning necessary during the period immediately following the award of a contract and addresses how the key operation issues involved are planned. Specific planning techniques are not covered.

7.1. *Post award planning*

As indicated earlier, pre-tender planning is normally carried out under considerable pressure of time, with resources sometimes necessarily spread over more than one concurrent tender or offer. There is, consequently, an element of the best being the enemy of the good, and acceptance that a practical and sensible method, once established, must suffice. There is, accordingly, after award a need and an opportunity to look at basic assumptions afresh.

Contract documents frequently call for submission of a formal programme within a stated period after award. The contractor's post-tender planning produces such a programme, but it needs to be produced more urgently and to be more detailed and comprehensive. As part of this process the contractor is likely to wish to make a review and analysis of the tender price and to sweep up any errors (hopefully, minor) made in the haste of tendering. Beyond this, the process should incorporate the latest and more fully considered information on the main contract assets of finance, human resources, equipment and materials.

This review planning also offers an opportunity to consider any alternatives to design, materials or construction methods which could not be pursued during the tender planning, although ideas for such alternatives can continue to surface later during construction.

From the contractor's viewpoint such alternatives either allow it to perform the works still in conformity with design and specification, but with a saving in performance cost to the contractor, or require acceptance of a change in design or specification, providing the client with either an improvement in finished work or a reduction in price, with the contractor expecting to receive some benefit from the necessary negotiation of varied rates.

Some contract documents, including those of the US Corps of Engineers, make specific provision for sharing of any benefits arising from such initiative by the contractor.

This planning is not a one-off operation but should continue, and continue to be reviewed, in the light of ongoing monitoring, more or less formally throughout the duration of the contract. Where the process is formalised, the information provided to the project manager may include a site cost provision bill based on the BOQ and a project management manual.

A site cost provision bill may be based on the BOQ analysis produced for the tender, after extracting any elements, including head office overheads and profit, which are not within the command of the project team. A project management manual, in effect, combines the project programme with a reasonably detailed method statement including: staffing, construction plant selection and financial schedules of production and earnings, costs and cash flow. These documents will be reviewed, revised and reissued progressively at intervals throughout the contract. This enables actual costs to be compared with planned costs and progressively incorporates information on project performance.

The specific techniques of planning do not differ significantly between work in the UK and that overseas, and consequently are not paraded here. Generally, however, temporary works and preliminaries are more significant in relation to the planning of the overseas project, than is the case in the UK.

There does, however, seem to be an essential difference between heavy civil engineering and building work. In civil engineering work, items are small in number and overlap in time and proceed concurrently. In building or other forms of engineering work, items are more diverse, separate and shorter in duration. In heavy civil construction a major contract may well number less than 100 significant activities. There is a school of thought which contends that a linked, activity bar-chart with resource levelling is preferable to sophisticated programming tools. A related school contends that neither resources nor calculated outputs are entirely inflexible and that if a critical task is tending to overrun, an alternative to re-scheduling is to move over a key general foreman to kick it into shape.

7.2. Planning of resources

Project financing

From a contractor's viewpoint there are two levels of financing

(a) the provision of funding to enable the project to be started
(b) the availability of funding to the contractor to meet oper-

ating contract costs, which in the mobilisation and first stage of construction may well exceed actual contract receipts.

The cost of the project may be funded by the client from its own resources, provided by an international agency or supportive government or arranged by the contractor under some form of finance and construct package. Where the country's currency is not freely exchangeable, there may be a further variant where the client produces local currency funding but requires funding either from an external source or through the contractor for offshore currency costs. It is usual, where the local currency is not freely exchangeable, for the contract terms to provide that payments to the contractor are made, in fixed proportions, partly in local currency and partly in a nominated offshore currency, usually at a rate of exchange fixed for the contract.

Where, as a facet of marketing, the contractor offers a package including finance, and such an offer proceeds to contract, the contractor will usually include a banker in its project consortium. The banker would assemble and organise such finance, which may comprise elements of bilateral aid and/or soft loan, supplemented by commercial loans.[63,72,74] The commercial element of such funding will require acceptable guarantees of repayment which may be tied to future proceeds from usage of the project.

Alternatively, as noted earlier, other unpledged client's assets may be used as surety. If a government or quasi-government agency is the client, the surety may be afforded by a central bank guarantee. Alternatively, surety may be afforded by assignment of future export products under a barter deal arrangement with the contractor or financing banker. Funding by an international agency is considered reasonably secure. When payment is financed directly by the client, the contractor will need to form a view of its continuing ability to meet all its contractual obligations on the due date. Where finance forms part of a package, the contractor is likely to have sufficient influence on disbursements to ensure that project payments are made. Wherever doubts as to the financial ability of the client arise the contractor will seek to insure through ECGD or suitable alternatives. The contractor will need to persuade the department that the project is viable and that the client's status is such that the guarantee premium is a fair assessment of the insurance risk of non-payment, or that the project is in the national interest, before cover will be granted. Difficulties may be experienced with ECGD when the local cost element is a high proportion of total project value.

Being reasonably satisfied on the supply of funds to the project and insured if necessary against ultimate failure to repay, the contractor's further concern is likely to be promptness of payment.

Traditional contracts require a cash input from the contractor at the beginning of the project, and hopefully break even during the contract working period, with any profit realised at the completion, and even then likely to be substantially or wholly tied up in the form of construction plant at its residual value. Many such contracts now provide mobilisation or plant advances against bonds, with progressive repayments during the contract to ease the contractor's initial cash flow position.

The maintenance of satisfactory cash flow is vital to the contractor, requiring the preparation of an initial cash flow forecast and its progressive monitoring and updating as an essential tool in project financial control. The first step of the payment chain is promptness of measurement and certification for work done, and it is in the contractor's best interest to establish mutual trust with the certifying engineer, thereby allowing measurement and certification to proceed concurrently. Measurements can then be submitted (if necessary with approximate on-account items included) certified and passed for payment, without delay at the end of each measurement period.

The balancing of cash inflow and outflow is essential for the contractor's survival and financial management of a contract, in which battle the contractually weaker parties can be most adversely affected and, accordingly, main contracts may include provision for prompt payment by the contractor to its subcontractors after receipt of certificate monies.

In spite of the best cash management it may still prove necessary to put significant funds into a project. These will then have to be provided either from any reserves the contractor may hold or from borrowing, principally from the contractor's banker. The banker may be prepared to treat a project loan as sufficiently secured by the signed contract and the contractor's reputation, but this is becoming increasingly unusual. With project loans being treated effectively as general overdraft, demands on the contractor's ability to provide tangible collateral security have become seriously compounded by the concurrent tendency (commented on earlier) of banks demanding similar 100% security cover for contract bonding exposure.

Where local currency is required in a country whose currency is not readily negotiable, it is usually possible to arrange a local currency overdraft against the security of a back-to-back deposit in an offshore branch of the same bank. This procedure obviates the need to import currency and subsequent problems of reconversion.

Human resources
The human resources available to, and used by a contractor in the performance of a project comprise some, or all of,

- UK project management staff seconded to site, or in support in head office
- indigenous staff and workforce of the country in which the project is performed
- third nation staff and workforce, recruited and imported to supplement the two previous categories
- subcontractors.

The divisions between these components are not entirely rigid, some UK staff may be nationals of other European or Commonwealth countries or third world nationals, perhaps recruited to earlier projects and groomed within the company. Subcontractors may range from technical specialists, with their own technicians, to local labour supply contractors; essentially, subcontractors are used when cost effective, that is when they can perform better and/or cheaper than could the contractor directly.

The project environment will influence the balance of these four components and vary enormously with the state of development, general standard of education and general culture of the country concerned. Some examples may illustrate the point. In the oil producing countries of the Middle East there are highly capable and educated people who are not available for recruitment to construction work because the culture and range of other employment opportunities downgrades construction as a potential source of employment. In the Indian subcontinent there are large numbers of well qualified and capable administrative and technical staff, but there is held to be a dearth of driving, sharp end, foremen. This gap is particularly sensitive since it may be contended that the choice of a general foreman is second only to that of a project manager in ensuring the success of a project.

Expatriates

A contractor has to make its own judgement of the posts which can be filled by local staff or by expatriates in each case and the quality and selection of key UK site management are generally accepted as crucial to the running of the project.[15,16,47,64,75]

There are certain guidelines.

(*a*) The project manager should be from within the company and well-known to the head office. Certain characteristics should be evident
  (i) reciprocal trust and easy communication with head office
  (ii) previous senior experience of working overseas and of managing relationships with expatriate and local personnel
  (iii) experience of managing organisations, and
  (iv) skill in relating to the local community.

Should the project manager need training or management development in these areas this should be arranged prior to the project commencing.

(*b*) Local staff should be used as much as possible. Usually local staff are less costly to the project than expatriates and, where the company sees a prospect of continuing activity in the area, should be selected, trained, groomed and absorbed into the company culture for higher things in the future.

(*c*) The best staff should be hired even if they are expensive. Where expatriates are required, the associated costs including costs of living and travel are high and, where possible, it pays to buy quality. An expatriate seen by local staff as highly paid, but who is clearly not up to the job is an embarrassment. However, more expatriates fail by personality, personal relations and inability to adapt to local conditions. Relatively seldom are their failures through lack of knowledge, experience, technical or professional skill.

The quality of expatriate staff has been said to be[64] a composition of

o honesty   o a liking for hard work
o sociability   o adaptability
o a sense of humour and   o at least average competence.

The incentives of staff on overseas projects combine (usually) higher salaries than at home, (usually) the opportunity to take on more responsibility sooner than at home and the possible satisfaction of a taste for travel, challenge or adventure.

An obvious issue is that of families. The social environment of a construction project in different cultures and customs presents its own challenges to family life. Other issues of climate, accommodation, health, educational and other facilities are also key elements of employment conditions. Some projects are close to towns, many so isolated that virtually all facilities have to be provided as part of the project. Some spouses are willing or even anxious to share pioneering conditions but less willing that their children should do so.

Some employees accept the conditions of overseas work in order to afford to send children to boarding school. Others accept boarding schools in order to be able to continue to live and work overseas. Alternatively, some accept that wife and children remain in the UK, apart from possible short visits, while yet others decide that when their children reach the age they consider critical (this may vary with the individual), they are no longer available.for work overseas.

Expatriate staff are provided by assignment of existing company staff, supplemented as necessary by recruitment. Where staff unproved by previous overseas experience are recruited, they need to be selected as much for apparent motivation and likely ability to adapt to site conditions and local culture as for apparent professional ability. It is of first importance in selection that sufficient attention is given to the match between the individual and social environment of the work area.

Local workforce and third nation employees

The possibilities of local recruitment are dictated by the assessment made of the local employment market. It is likely that economics will, in most areas, dictate the maximum use of local manpower. It is also likely that either the terms of the contract or the culture of the project will encourage the provision of opportunities for job training and job development. If the contractor foresees a continuing activity in the area then the benefits of such training are obvious. Training provided for a one-off project may be less cost-effective to the contractor and frustrating for the individual who has been trained only to find limited opportunities to use new skills.

The initial recruitment of local employees by a contractor new to an area has to be made by expatriate staff, who may themselves be new to the area, and has to be made quickly. The arrangements for obtaining applicants may be more or less sophisticated, depending on the area, and ranging from newspaper advertising to a personal call on a local village headman. Selection from those offering may well be complicated by differences of language and culture. Good advice, particularly from a reliable local agent, is invaluable. Bad advice leads to the engagement of friends, relations or, on occasions, those offering an appropriate inducement; any such faulty appointments can take time to discover and remedy. As in many other matters, much depends on the experience, instinct and quality of the designated project manager.

Recruitment from a third nation is considered where a local workforce is not available; or where the contractor considers that externally recruited workers would, by their greater skills and efficiency, be more cost effective than local recruits. These considerations may apply to virtually the whole of the workforce or only to certain trades. The possibility of introducing third country workers naturally depends on any relevant regulations and may require a formal license. It may also be subject to special terms of the contract conditions. During the Middle East oil boom period India, Pakistan and Sri Lanka were the principal catchment areas with contractors recruiting through agents based in Bombay, Karachi and Colombo. Other major recruitment areas now active include Thailand, the Philippines and Turkey. As with most other operations the choice of source area, the selection of a recruiting agent and the establishment of procedures for selection and recruitment benefit from as much time and consideration as possible. The more preparation there is before contract award, the more reliable the operation is likely to be.

A contractor is likely to select a recruiting agent, either in response to unsolicited approaches, or on advice, recommendation or introduction. Alternatively, the contractor can visit the recruiting area, taking the best advice available there, perhaps including the UK Embassy or High Commission before making a choice. Almost certainly, it will arrange for a senior expatriate to take part in the selection process in the country of recruitment before any worker is engaged, and to supervise the arrangements for passages and any necessary medical or immigration processes. Each recruit is likely to be engaged on an individual contract, for a fixed period, subject to renewal or termination terms and including accommodation, messing and return transport upon completion.

Subcontractors
The organisational arrangements between main contractor and subcontractor are highly varied.

At the one extreme, a subcontractor is effectively a member of a consortium, assembled and led by the contractor to tender or to submit a proposal for negotiated work. Such a link is unlikely to be broken during the contract, although either party may seek to modify its terms as the project proceeds.

Next is a potential subcontractor, whose offer formed the basis of the contractor's tender. There is unlikely to be a binding formal agreement between the two parties prior to the contractor's submission of the tender; either due to shortage of time or to one or both parties thinking it may be in a stronger negotiating position after the award. Either or both parties may then seek an improvement in terms once an award is announced. During this stage an alternative subcontractor may be chosen.

Finally, subcontractors are not involved before tender, but are engaged later for work which the contractor either proposed to perform directly or treated as a potential subcontract in the estimate. These could well include local contractors for temporary works. The balancing and marshalling of these various human resources are vital elements of the preliminary stages of the contractor's performance of the project.

Equipment

An outline selection of equipment is made as part of the pre-tender planning. While establishing provisional equipment prices and availability some agreement would be reached with potential suppliers.

Post award planning, in which the plant department plays a major role, must now define the construction methods to be used, the equipment available from the company's fleet, and thus the additional equipment needed. This may be obtained by purchase new, or used, or leased, and it can be obtained within the country of operation (either locally manufactured or through importing agents), in the UK, or on the world market. In a plant intensive contract, where equipment costs are a high proportion of total costs, it is not unknown for a highly favourable equipment deal to be sufficient to sway the balance between alternative methods for a major operation. This may necessitate replanning of part or the whole of the works.

Financial factors to be considered in the plant selection decision include

- ownership cost to the contract; purchase price less foreseen residual ownership or disposal value
- effect on cash flow; influenced by whether the equipment is new or second hand, by whether it is bought or leased, by any deferred payment terms negotiable, and by any advance payment in the contract terms
- effect of taxes, duties or other imposts
- the operating cost (to the contract) in operators, fuel and consumables and the costs of maintenance and breakdown spares and fitters.

The contractor will need to ask several questions.

- Will each particular piece of equipment deliver the required output?
- Will it be available in time?
- Can it be supplied from stock or does it have to be made or assembled?
- How reliable is it?

- What percentage utilisation can be expected?
- What is the availability and delivery of spares?
- What items of spares need to be carried as site stock?
- How readily and how quickly will a manufacturer's fitter be provided to site if needed?
- Can the equipment be operated, serviced, maintained and repaired by the quality of fitters who can be recruited locally, or trained within the time available?
- Do expatriate fitters and operators need to be provided?

A balance has to be made between all these factors, including all the sourcing options before choosing any alternative construction methods. An allowance for knock-on effects of breakdowns (where one piece of equipment may be unable to work if another is broken down) needs to be made. Choosing smaller items of plant may allow this to be largely overcome by overtime working.

Plant decisions need to be made quickly to allow firm orders to be placed so that equipment can reach site in time. The key figure, though not the sole arbiter, is likely to be the company plant manager. To fulfil this function, the plant manager needs to judge, based on experience, the site performance and maintenance requirement of equipment from each major manufacturer. Computer technology can assist in profiling the utility of individual pieces of plant and make information more readily accessible, but personal experience is the crucial element. However, such experience may well carry some prejudice based on an untypical past occurrence.

Most plant managers will have a preferred manufacturer for each type of equipment and one or more manufacturers previously found unsatisfactory and discarded. They will seek continually to maintain and improve access to the preferred manufacturers. Future directed plant managers will also be looking beyond these established preferences in case things might be changing.

For major imported equipment, the contractor is buying in bulk on a world market and would expect to be able to do so more cost effectively than by purchasing locally. The contractor may find that local agencies have been granted exclusive purchasing rights which restrict alternative buyers access to the supplier. In some instances compensation is payable to the local agent for not using its services.

113

Materials

Materials for a major project are likely to comprise

- site produced materials
- locally purchased manufactured materials
- imported manufactured materials.

The contractor will have assembled information on the sources, quality, availability and prices of principal materials as part of the pre-tender assessment. This information is now reviewed, to confirm these sources, and set in train the mechanism for purchase and delivery.

For most construction projects, the main site produced materials are common or selected fills, structural, granular components from sands or crushed stone, concrete or asphalt aggregates. On most major projects in the developing world all of these are directly site won, or site manufactured, or produced through subcontractors who may require some degree of technical assistance or supervision. Haulage costs are a substantial element of total delivered material costs, and, so, judicious location of the quarries and borrow pit can assist the control of the number and costs of the vehicles required.

The quality of the site produced materials is important and proving the quality means establishing that the material will meet the specification. Specifications are often carried forward from one area to another, and it may be that no practically obtainable site produced materials meet the specification as written. In such a case, the contractor has contracted to perform the virtually impossible and, consequently, it is not well placed to negotiate a variation to the specification or design to resolve the problem.

In other cases, the use of a more common material, or the use of a higher quality material, offers a benefit to the project. The contractor's experience may allow it to suggest specification and/or design changes in relation to the selection of materials or their performance. Such decisions will involve evaluating the particular climatic conditions or other circumstances of the area of work against which the client or its engineer may be willing to consider accepting the proposed changes. Aspects of the work which may offer such opportunity could include fill quality, granular pavement or foundation layers, asphalt and concrete mixes.

Locally purchased manufactured materials are either locally manufactured or imported for sale by local merchants or agents. The possibility of supply from such sources, which should have been investigated in the pre-tender assessment, needs to be reviewed and confirmed. For locally manufactured items, the contractor requires economy, acceptable quality and reliability of supply. The contractor may be able to contribute to quality and reliability of supply by entering into an arrangement with a local supplier to provide equipment, additional management or supervision. Should such arrangements happen they need to be mutually advantageous. The contractor may also seek to negotiate design or specification changes to allow the fullest use of locally manufactured materials.

For imported materials, the contractor will generally buy on the world market. Provisional prices and delivery dates will have been obtained for tender purposes and confirmation is required, often with negotiated improved terms, with the extant or competing supplier. Usually the contractor's position in any such negotiation is stronger once a contract is awarded. The reverse position may apply, however, in respect of scarce materials, a sellers' market or monopoly conditions. The contractor needs to assess such possibilities before tender and, accordingly, seek to make the commitment of its provisional arrangements with suppliers more or less binding.

The complement of such purchasing decisions are the associated transport arrangements and the requirement for storage arrangements and facilities, to be considered later.

8

Project management

8.1. Doing the work

At this stage, the contract is awarded, the resources needed have been assessed and the post-tender planning initiated. These activities prepare for the execution of the contract. An overseas project organisation is geographically distant from head office and necessarily has a high degree of autonomy. This makes appropriate measures for integration of vital importance and some of these measures are highlighted in the subsequent sections on culture, style and welfare; relationships; manpower; and monitoring and record. The reported preparations for a major military engagement[76] have common ground with those for setting up a major construction project. Issues of logistics, communications, accommodation, personal relations and team building, and consideration for local custom and sensibilities have to be addressed.

Culture, style and welfare

Culture and style are crucial both to the way the project operates and to its relationships with the local environment.[20,30,36,77-80] Every project has a culture and style. This may evolve without conscious development. In some cases, it is claimed that the traditions and homogeneity of the contracting company are so strong that all its senior members will know what is expected of them and act accordingly. The contention here is that, generally, reliance should not be placed on the most advantageous culture and style just happening; intentional development of these factors is worthwhile and can contribute to the performance of the project.

The contractor's objectives will include performance to time, quality and profit. In most cases, it will include more. The company's aims, which were considered earlier, may include the retention, grooming and development of staff, so as to consolidate its position in the country and enhance its reputation. Inevitably, the objectives will develop as the project proceeds and by interaction between the project and the local community the desired culture and style of the project will emerge. Such critical issues may also dictate the strategy and structure of the project organisation. These ticklish negotiations need to involve the project manager, the local agent and the community.

What kind of project?
In most successful overseas projects task orientation is dominant but carries with it a high degree of people orientation, in that the task is best achieved by a well selected, integrated and motivated team who are sufficiently well looked after to be able to give a high degree of commitment to the task. The style of management also needs to accommodate the differing cultures of the local and European employees, and any immigrant workers who may have traditions of more or less authoritarian relationships.

The essentials would seem to be clear aims, an appropriate organisation structure and style, quality staff, wise selection and effective leadership by the project manager. Very different styles of leadership have proved equally effective on different projects and it may be that the best results are achieved by a project manager with sufficient confidence to express his own personality and adapt, as necessary, to circumstances rather than seek to ape a model.

There may be external constraints on the way the project develops. The client or the funding agency may have preempted some decisions. The project residential camp site may be allocated, dictating separation from, rather than integration with, the local community. It may be shared with the client's and engineer's staff with joint facilities provided, which may influence the contractor's decision as to whether staff can be accompanied by their families. Climate and conditions may be unsuitable for families.

The decision as to whether expatriate staff can be accompanied by families clearly affects the culture of the project. Some potential staff will not accept an appointment if unaccompanied. For others there are differing views as to whether they perform more effectively with or without families. The presence of families influences temporary work requirements, and the possible degree and kind of interrelation with the local community.

From the contractor's viewpoint welfare begins with its expatriate staff, their families at site, locally recruited staff and immigrant workforce. To a greater or lesser degree, it may extend to the locally recruited workforce, to the local community and to the families of expatriate staff left in the UK. Its scope depends on needs, local conditions, any relevant requirements of the contract, the project culture, the degree of integration with the local community and the contractor's aims and objectives.

Keeping employees reasonably healthy and fed so that they are able to work is critical. In some cases that is all; the deliberate philosophy is to pay well, provide frequent leaves and drive employees as hard as possible between leaves. More likely, is a degree of care for any expatriate families so that expatriate employees are not distracted from work by worrying about them. The provision of recreational facilities in the hope that these will improve health and morale and so enhance performance is an oft used ploy. Occasionally, the contractor seeks to establish a position in the local community, to win goodwill and to improve local relationships. It may act altruistically by contributing to, or providing some facilities for, the local community.

The project manager is necessarily at the centre of all these judgements. One, on a large and, ultimately, highly successful project, made his apologies to a member of the consultant's staff 'I'm afraid you won't see much of me on site; a project manager's job is to see that wives get the right coloured paint on their walls; the rest can be delegated'.

Relationships

The connection between the project and the company's head office is central to considerations of human resources, corporate style and project structure. These will influence the nature of the relationship with the community, local agent and/or partner, the client and its consultant or supervising engineer. All of these relationships need to be nurtured. How these relationships can be developed will have been the subject of pre-tender activity and the process of fostering harmonious terms will be started by the contractor's representatives when undertaking site visits prior to the job starting. While the contractor may be clear on what it wants, each relationship has two parties. A consensual relationship is difficult to establish if the other party believes in constructive tension.

The project manager with the contractor's local agent and/or partner will do all they can to foster and develop the desired relationships. One contractor's approach to the supervising engineer was simple, ' If we work together the job will succeed and we can then fight over the apportionment of credit, if we concentrate on opposing each other, it will fail and we can then fight over the apportionment of blame '. That contract succeeded.

Individual personalities are important; initial apparent incompatibilities can sometimes be resolved by patience and by care to demonstrate good faith and good intentions. Sometimes they can be resolved by intervention, perhaps by the individual who made the initial visits and contacts. Sometimes they are too deep seated, and so clearly harmful to ongoing relationships that one or both parties have to be removed.

Beyond the individuals are the corporate relationships. At the end of the day, these are likely to be governed by the prospect of benefit. In accordance with the maxim that a contract must offer benefit to both parties to be acceptable, if the contractor, the client and the local community can all foresee benefit from the current and future projects there is an incentive to continue relationships.

Such continuity would involve the extended stay in the area of the contractor's establishment and in all probability of some of its staff. Once this is the accepted prospect, the logic of seeking to improve relationships between the organisations and between individuals begins to seem compelling.

8.2. Mobilisation and logistics

Finance, manpower, equipment and materials now need to be mobilised.

Finance

The contractor needs to mobilise finance in local currency and in readily convertable offshore currency. If the local currency is not freely exchangeable, the contractor will wish to avoid being left with a residue of this currency on completion of the contract and, as noted, can, in some cases, achieve this by arranging a local currency overdraft, guaranteed by a back-to-back offshore currency deposit.

The first step must be to open a local bank account, either in the national main financial area or in the nearest sufficiently large town to the project site. The bank chosen is likely to be one with close links to the contractor's UK bank. The information governing this choice will have been obtained earlier. In practice, there is in all developing countries either a branch of an international bank or a local bank with some ties to an international bank. The next stage is to make money available to the project. Whether it is funded by the client or by an international agency, there is likely to be provision for project advances, and the contractual formalities to obtain these need to be completed as early as possible. If these payments are in a mix of local and offshore currency the contractor will nominate its local account and one or more offshore accounts to receive payment. Often the contractor has, as a measure of prudence, erred on the side of overestimating the offshore element, and may during the project require to top-up the local funding by cash transfer or by overdraft.

The contractor, if party to the project financing, should have ensured that the finance package disbursements are phased so that the project construction is very close to being continuously cash-positive. The design of the disbursement arrangements should prevent undue delay or diversion of funds to other needs of the client. If the project funding is not continuously cash-positive, the contractor must make such arrangements to allocate other funds or to activate overdraft arrangements.

By some or other of these means the contractor will provide that both local and offshore funds are available to meet project expenditure, while exercising a careful credit control in relation to debtors and creditors.

Manpower
The first mobilisation of human resources effectively took place with the assignment of one or more members of the project co-ordination section of the UK office to the tender or offer team. These individuals are, then, the nucleus of the UK based project team and will have worked with the engineering, plant and materials departments, and the designated project manager and/or senior site staff on the post award planning and mobilisation.

The site team come next. It is important that the team should include all the necessary talents. The qualities required range from political and presentational skills, commerce and negotiation, man management and personal relations, to technical construction experience, flair and innovation, enthusiasm and charisma, commitment and persistence. As far as possible these qualities are needed at site but the UK office is part of the project team and missing elements can be made up, on a visit basis, by UK office members or, when necessary, by outside experts. Supplementing, but also sharing and overlapping these management skills, are the UK supervisors and working foremen of the team. The numbers in which they are required are obviously subject to the availability of trade skills in the indigenous and/or third nation workforce. Essentially, their role is to ensure that construction work is performed as efficiently as possible with the available workforce. To this end, craft skills are taught hands-on to carefully chosen unskilled workers. By establishing a close working accord with their workers they provide an indispensable input to project motivation. Efforts to save UK expatriate costs by covering these functions either by UK technical management, or by highly intelligent and technically trained indigenous and third world staff often prove disappointing.[58]

Almost inevitably, the organisation structure of the project is a matrix. Site staff are responsible to and through the project manager, however functional lines of the matrix facilitate management processes and are cultivated. These functional lines reflect the common activity, language and expertise of departmental specialists, in the UK and on site, and are strengthened where these specialists have worked together on previous projects. These specialist cultures are deliberately cultivated by staff visits to the UK office on leave and by UK staff visits to site.

It is usual and useful to attempt a family tree organisation chart, but it is essential to realise that project staff are individuals and that, by the time they reach site, they are difficult to exchange. It is often easier to modify the chart to accommodate the individual than vice versa, and a member who disappoints in one role may (particularly, perhaps, in the case of a local recruit) prove valuable when given a second chance in a slightly different function. The essential is to establish as effective and smoothly running a team as possible, as early as possible.

The key figure must be the project manager. Some of the requirements for this role have been considered. The individual appointed should satisfy as many of these as possible, and must have sufficient ability and achievement record to command necessary respect. Supermen are rare but the project manager and UK management should realise and acknowledge their limitations and structure the project team to utilise known strengths and to provide support where needed. One project manager may concentrate on a hands-on driving of site production; another on administration, or on maintaining and enhancing project relationships. All these are important contributions. The project manager should be able to design the project management structure so that they do what they do best—which is often also what is enjoyable—delegating, but controlling, the rest.

The project manager may have been part of the project team before the award or, if not, should become a part of it as soon after award as possible. As part of the induction, the project manager should, usually, be taken to the site and introduced to important local contacts by the local agent and the senior manager who has established the company's presence in the region. The project manager should take some time to initiate the development of ongoing site relationships.

It may not be necessary that the project manager should remain permanently in the project area at this stage; there are useful contributions to be made elsewhere. Importing materials and equipment, or the recruitment of third nation employees, planning and mobilisation in the home office, development and clarification of the project objectives and the selection, assignment and recruiting of UK staff may all command time. Some staff can serve little useful purpose until some related element of mobilisation is in position, perhaps the arrival of equipment. As a general rule they should not arrive at site, before they can be usefully employed, while wives or families should not arrive before they can be assimilated without undue stresses to themselves or to the project operation. The numerical requirements for UK staff, indigenous employees, third nation employees and subcontractors are initially established, at this stage, by post award planning. These numbers are not immutable and need to be constantly reviewed as the project proceeds; poor productivity may demand additional personnel or accelerated acquisition of skills by indigenous employees may reduce the demand for expatriates.

The selection and induction of indigenous and third nation personnel will need to be timed so that pre-production training can be slotted in. The project manager must oversee the arrangements and may participate directly in recruitment in the country of operation and/or in the third nation recruiting centres. All due care must be exercised in learning and complying with official regulations or customs for employment and/or for immigration. Relations with unions or similar organisations need to be carefully managed. In all likelihood there will be an attempt to extract a greater degree of compliance from a newly arrived contractor who is in a hurry, than prevails elsewhere in the employment market. Conversely, an experienced contractor may exploit weaknesses in the bargaining power of labour and usurp their organisations.

The logistics of moving personnel to site depend entirely on the project location and the communications system of the area. Generally, all personnel from the UK or a third world nation are flown to the nearest airport to the project. This involves a relatively small exercise in arranging flights, visas and medical requirements for UK staff and families, but a larger one in third nation recruiting. There are still some opportunities for other transport; for example, dhows across the Gulf to Middle East projects. The move from airport to port to the project may still involve considerable distances by truck or four-wheel drive.

Site administration

Establishing the framework for site administration is a vital element of project mobilisation and includes

- o the setting up of a measurement, payment and accounting system
- o the operation of the personnel department
- o medical and welfare issues
- o materials and equipment stores, stocks issues and records
- o secretarial and records systems.

It must be designed to utilise the resources available, which may offer a small number of lowly paid but highly competent clerks, or a high number with less competence; or may indicate computerisation, either because trained or readily trainable operators are available, or simply because clerical staff are virtually unobtainable.

Equipment

At this stage, construction equipment has been selected for the project and the most favourable supply prices and conditions negotiated by the company plant department. Funds for purchase or leasing will have been made available from plant advances provided under the contract. This position is considered to be reasonably final, although it is accepted that developments during the project, such as failure to achieve planned progress, or an instruction to include additional work, may necessitate the purchase of additional items.

There is usually, at this point, one plant item or group of items whose delivery is critical to overall programming. On a heavy civil engineering construction project needing large volumes of concrete or asphalt this may well be the quarry crushing equipment required to produce aggregates. This equipment may be available within the contractor's equipment fleet or purchased, second hand or off the shelf, from the manufacturer. In many cases, it may have to be designed and fabricated from standard units to meet the particular requirements of the project and the proposed stone source. If so, delay in shipping may be expected. This may call for further modification of the programme, or it may be possible to avoid this by stop gap purchase of a less favourable aggregate, by incentives to the manufacturer to expedite delivery, or by faster means of transport to site.

Subject to such modifications, firm orders are now placed for equipment to be purchased in accordance with the construction programme. Arrangements for payment and forwarding to site need to be put in hand. The construction equipment market is worldwide and the contractor may well obtain plant from the UK, from other European countries, the USA or Japan. If second-hand equipment is envisaged then used plant sales in the Middle East or other centres of construction activity are an option. Finally, purchase from manufacturers or stockholders in the country of operations is a possibility.

Most forwarding of equipment for overseas projects is by sea. A contractor may make all forwarding arrangements entirely in-house, but he is more likely to engage a shipping agent. Then the manufacturer will usually provide delivery to docks, the shipping agent will arrange loading, provision and forwarding of bills of lading, carriage to port of destination and offloading. The contractor will arrange port clearance and inland transport from port to project site. Depending on the size and nature of the equipment, the type of shipping available, and the facilities on the ship and at the port of destination, the equipment may be carried as a complete unit, or broken down for transit. It may travel as hold cargo, deck cargo or on a ro-ro (roll on, roll off) basis for wheeled units.

The contractor's arrangements for inland transport depend on distance between port and project site, the availability and condition of roads and/or rail or water transport facilities. The contractor must investigate these alternatives, satisfy himself on the information given; for instance, the clearances of bridges if rail transport exists, the condition of roads and the availability and carrying capacity of river or coastal waterborne transport. It will probably need to include one or more low loaders in the equipment supply and may well have to provide teams grading tracks or simply filling potholes to maintain access.

Alternatives need to be kept constantly in mind. Road transport to the Middle East or road ferry transport to North Africa may bypass shipping difficulties, while the limited use of air freight for smaller, infrequently required spares may allow advantageous savings in cost of spares held and in stores costs.

Materials

The supply and forwarding arrangements for imported materials largely reflect those for equipment. Again, the market is worldwide, the contractor will place orders as most favourable to the contract in terms of quality, cost and delivery, and will be likely to use the same shipping agent, and to meet similar problems in inland transport to site.

There are naturally some other problems. There may be no local supply of cement, bitumen and fuel; in which case these are simply additional imported materials to be dealt with accordingly. In other cases, however, these commodities are nominally available in the country; either imported by a national agency, or manufactured or processed in the country. Dangers arise when they do not meet international standards of quality, consistency or reliability of supply. On occasion they can cost more than they would if imported, but the contractor may or may not be permitted to import directly. Transport of bitumen is either drummed, requiring decanting at site, or bulk, requiring heated transport and storage. While equipment transport is concentrated in the earlier stages, materials supply and transport must continue throughout the project.

There are also site produced materials, particularly stone aggregates and other granular materials. After proving sources and arranging access, the contractor needs to establish hard rock or gravel quarries and to provide, install and operate crushing and screening plants. This can be done either independently, as part of the project temporary works, or in some form of association, upgrading and controlling the operations of a local quarry operator. A discussion of the issues of materials quality control, contractor proposed alternative or substitute materials, and of concrete and asphalt mixing plants as a further part of the temporary works fall within other sections.

Temporary works

For a major third world construction project in an isolated area temporary works are usually a major undertaking.

They may include any, or all, of

o road access to site
o rail spur extensions or sidings

o temporary river or coastal wharves
o covered and open storage
o materials stockpiling and reclamation provisions
o offices and workshops
o quarry crushing and screening plant
o concrete and/or asphalt mixing plants
o accommodation for staff, families and workforce
o hospital
o medical facilities
o school
o club and recreational facilities
o food supplies
o water supply
o electricity supply
o connection to telephone system or wireless.

The extent of such provision in any project depends on a number of factors including

o the size and duration of the project
o its location
o the existence and quality of any local facilities
o the presence or absence of expatriate wives and families
o the degree of integration of the project into the local community.

The staff of the client and/or its engineer are likely to require facilities corresponding to some of the above. In some cases these are treated entirely separately, in others there is seen to be advantage in combining facilities. In some cases the contract demands that some facilities, which will be required by the client, are provided on an ongoing basis. Such facilities may be constructed early on for use by the contractor during the construction period. Normally, a substantial element of temporary works construction is required by the contractor in the early stages. Site accommodation offices and workshops are likely to be the first requirements and can be largely prefabricated, as caravans or Portakabins, or provided in sections for rapid and easy site assembly. If suitable local contractors exist, the erection of these buildings can, in some cases, be subcontracted. Balancing the work necessary to finish temporary works and the mobilisation of staff and workforce to arrive as soon as there is work for them to do and sufficient facilities to allow them to do it, is an essential element of pre-construction planning.

8.3. Motivation and performance

The motivation of individuals on the project needs to be driven by the fulfilment of the project objectives. The motivation affects the contractor's site staff, be they from the UK, indigenous to the country or third nation. The motivation of head office staff needs to be considered alongside that of the site staff and this joint motivation is strengthened by the links between site and head office. Senior site staff on a first contract in an area are usually from the UK but may include expatriates of other nationalities, possibly promoted within and integrated into the organisation on previous projects. Where the contractor is maintaining a continuing presence in an area, there may equally be indigenous staff similarly promoted and integrated.

The motivation of such senior staff is crucial. Projects have gone sour where conditions have been uncomfortable, and expatriate staff have subconsciously convinced themselves that they are doing sufficient by simply staying there and surviving.

There are recurring patterns. Where the performance of a project is going badly, dissatisfaction spreads and there are continual minor complaints; with a project going well satisfaction spreads and complaints are fewer; and of course in a winning project there tends to be a little money available to attempt to deal with such complaints as do occur. Normally at the beginning of a project there are new factors, not fully foreseen, introducing difficulties which require extreme effort to overcome in order to achieve programme performance. If these challenges are met then momentum is generated, often leading to further improvement on programmed performance.

There are the maintenance or hygiene factors of motivation.[81] Staff must be adequately fed, housed and paid and the needs of their families reasonably provided for. Beyond this, UK expatriates on overseas construction, or at home, are motivated by the prospect of career advancement, but more generally by job satisfaction, individual pride in achievement and

128

pride in the company's achievement. Even higher salaries, although sometimes individually bargained for with considerable tenacity, are appreciated not only as money, but also as confirmation that the company buys from the top of the barrel.

When some of the UK staff and all other staff are newly recruited, creating the project culture which spreads this motivation to such new recruits is invaluable.

For indigenous or third nation staff on continuing employment with the company, remuneration is usually significantly higher than in their home economy and this is a major factor in creating a motivated workforce. Nevertheless, pride in achievement seems equally important. A sense of being accepted and absorbed as wholly part of the company seems of comparable importance.

At workforce level hygiene factors are again important, but pride in achievement and in membership of a winning team can often be very obvious and contribute greatly to performance. UK expatriate foremen excel at engendering this spirit.

The desire to succeed is perhaps more evident in overseas construction than in most employment. The task is the purpose. At its simplest 'if we're not going to do it well, why aren't we somewhere else?' is a question which many will ask of themselves.

The building blocks should now come together

o a contract won or negotiated on viable terms
o clear project objectives
o good pre-construction planning
o sufficient project finance
o the right equipment and spares backup
o the right materials
o a well chosen and balanced team who are well motivated.

Performance should follow. In practice problems, not fully foreseen, arise and are only contained and overcome by constant flexibility, replanning, peering ahead, watching, monitoring, coaxing and, in less enlightened cultures, pushing and cursing.

If they are overcome, as they should be, there will inevitably be more problems, but the pattern of success begins to be established and performance appears.

8.4. Quality management

Quality management is usually held to comprise quality control and quality assurance.[82–84]

Quality control is, essentially, ensuring that materials and components received at site, or won or produced at site, and finished construction work all satisfy the requirements specified in the contract documents. The procedures for this, basically similar to those for a UK project, are likely to include

(a) obtaining manufacturer's test certificates for main materials received. The contractor and the client's supervising engineer will each make their own judgement on the reliability of such certificates and may wish corroborative tests on site, or in a reliable independent laboratory. The process of quality control can be assisted by an inspection, at the works, of main components or manufactured materials by representatives of the contractor, the client's engineer, or an independent nominated inspector. Internationally acknowledged independent inspectors operate in most manufacturing countries. Such inspection is likely to include an overview of any testing for certificates.

(b) undertaking testing of materials won or produced at site, or components produced at site. The main materials are likely to include

- general or granular fills or foundation material
- stone aggregates
- asphalt
- concrete
- occasional site produced bricks and building blocks.

The contract usually defines in reasonable detail the required laboratory and testing equipment to be installed at site and operated by trained technicians. The sharing of testing facilities by the contractor and the client's engineer depend on mutual confidence and site relationships; there is usually some scope for discussion.

Similarly, the location and frequency of samples and the applicability of particular statistical procedures for evaluating results may be subject to negotiation. However, in most projects the contractor is committed to quality and, with reasonable relationships with the client and its engineer, good quality standards can be achieved provided good faith exists on all sides.

Quality Assurance (QA), as applied to overseas constructing operation, is similar to that seen in the UK. Be it home or away, QA is a mechanism for ensuring that the construction process takes place within the framework of a quality system. This quality system is a statement of how an international contractor or design practice undertakes its business in relationship to the quality of the output. A contractor operating in the international market will have a quality system which states how it manages the process of construction—this will be supported by a quality manual which catalogues descriptions, standards and procedures under the following headings

- o management responsibility
- o quality system
- o contract review
- o design control document control
- o purchasing
- o purchaser supplied products
- o product identification
- o and traceability
- o process control
- o inspection and testing
- o inspection, measuring and test equipment
- o inspection and test status
- o control of non-conforming product
- o corrective action
- o handling, storage, package and delivery
- o quality records
- o internal quality audits
- o training
- o servicing
- o statistical techniques.

Obviously not all of these requirements will fit the needs of individual international contractors—some will.

The manual produced for the project is a statement which identifies the action necessary for the construction to conform to the standards laid down in the International Standards 9000 (ISO 9000) document. The contractor can proceed to internal certification and, if the quality system is sufficiently robust, it may be Quality Assured.

Contracting organisations are increasingly adopting formalised quality assurance and seeking the relevant national or international certification, impelled by a belief in its cost effectiveness or its value as a marketing asset as potential clients become convinced of its virtues. The requirements for operating manuals are reasonably flexible and can conveniently be made compatible with individual project management manuals. The current concept of quality circles has long had its informal counterpart on overseas construction projects; in site cabins over a cup of tea or in the bar after work the day's doings or problems are discussed; someone remembers how something was done on an earlier project in a different country and wonders if it could be adapted to work. Many of these suggestions become more extravagant as the evening advances and are forgotten the next morning. Some are developed and adopted. A major benefit of a formal quality circle is held to be that it gives the workforce some measure of ownership of the workplace. A successful project culture would share this aim and often achieve it.

Dimensional control of line and level of construction

In this aspect a contract normally calls for strict conformance with the specification, lest work be condemned and replaced. Sometimes a financial penalty or additional work is demanded in cases where such failure is not significantly harmful to the performance and acceptability of the project. Clearly, the penalty should not be unreasonable; disputes delay progress. On borderline decisions good site relationships help to avoid disputes. A contractor may find it prudent to aim for an average quality above specified minima, by a margin sufficient to minimise borderline decisions and establish a measure of good faith. Such safety margins need to be achieved without excessive additional cost.

Less easily specified is good workmanship. This derives largely from the quality of trades foremen and their training, supervision and motivation of the trades workforce and, in the end, it is likely to reflect the mandated aims and the culture of the project. It is, in its turn, reflected in the long term performance of the works after completion, and in the client's satisfaction and the contractor's reputation.

8.5. Safety management

Overseas construction has a probably deservedly poor reputation for safety management. Local safety regulations, where they exist at all, may be imperfectly drafted and poorly enforced, and local compensation payments are likely to be comparatively low. An impoverished legislative framework may inculcate sets of values which accept risk taking on site. On sites where the culture of task achievement is dominant, an element of machismo may also induce a willingness to be seen to be taking risks. Against this background the appointment of a safety officer, if made at all, may be treated as a formality with the person nominated being either too junior or too committed to other duties to achieve anything.

If site safety is to be pursued effectively it must be an integral part of the project objective and safe attitudes a part of the project culture. Management at head office and at site must be seen to care. Then, and only then, will an effective and committed safety officer be appointed, and given sufficient call on time and resources to achieve results.

8.6. Performance of package projects

The preceding sections on performance have been directed to a project, substantially designed before award and by implication following the traditional pattern of design by a consultant, followed by tender, award and construction by a contractor.

Much of the content applies similarly to package projects but there are clearly important differences.

The sections on marketing cover alternative contractual relationships including the contractor as a project creator providing the client, by agreement and negotiation, with a package usually involving a one stop consortium of subcontract designers, specialist contractors and suppliers.

The advantages which are claimed for such arrangements include

(a) beneficial contract terms; such terms provide for interim review stages with an option for the client to terminate the contract as a result of such review. These reviews contribute to ensuring that risks are carried where they can best be borne and where they can be most effectively controlled.

(b) fast track construction; this would allow partial mobilisation and preliminary work by the contractor on preliminary design information before final design is completed. The main contractor and specialist subcontractors and suppliers can contribute to the development of design in the earlier stages. Thus widening the scope for a value engineering input.

(c) mobilisation of finance; this can be provided by the client or, as part of a package, by the contractor. Where the contractor provides finance, it will be party to the contract terms ensuring the availability of finance. This needs to be sufficiently flexible to meet incurred costs thus obviating advances from the client.

(d) mobilisation of human resources; this can conveniently begin earlier, in particular the project manager designate can ideally be a member of the project team from the design stage. Moreover, the teams responsible for initial temporary works can start early as can the selection and recruitment of indigenous personnel. Earlier starts allow time for more information and advice to be gathered and a more considered evaluation of this advice. This should lead to better personnel being selected.

(e) mobilisation of equipment; an early view can usually be formed on the equipment which is likely to be critical to mobilisation and for performance of the project. This view should be informed by the performance requirement of each piece of equipment so that manufacture or assembly can be put in hand in ample time. On less time-critical items the advantage is that negotiation with potential suppliers can start with each party knowing from the beginning that a successful negotiation is likely to mean a firm order. This usually produces a keener offer.

(f) mobilisation of materials; as for equipment, any foreseen bottlenecks due to long delivery for particular items can be eliminated by the client placing an advance order with a nominated supplier. Scarce materials can be designed out of the construction. Both parties can start negotiations reasonably expecting that, if successful, an order is likely to follow.

(g) temporary works; these can be designed early in the design process and constructed in phases, to match the progressive mobilisation of resources. This may reduce the contractor's reliance on prefabricated structures or on unsatisfactory local subcontractors.

(h) quality management; the input of the main contractor and of specialist subcontractors and suppliers is available to the design and planning team from the conceptual design stage. This enables design and programming decisions to be made with a reasonable prior knowledge of who the contractor is and its resources.

The early start can provide the time to create the quality plan and set up a quality system. Any prototypes or mock-ups can be tested in order to establish the benchmarks of quality that are required for key elements of the job.

8.7. Collecting rewards

Monitoring and recording

The project manager is at the sharp end of project performance, but the project should ultimately be controlled by head office management. To perform this function UK management must receive reports and records which allow them to monitor both performance and cost, and to intervene if and when necessary. Intervention would most likely take the form of additional support to the project manager. In a good relationship the project manager would be the first to know of the need for such support and would be able to ask for it. However, adequate monitoring ensures that the project is progressing smoothly and that the firm has selected the appropriate management team.

Such monitoring depends upon communication of reports and records from site to head office. This information will need to include data of relevance to functional departments. Needless to say the ease with which this information flows is greatly enhanced by senior head office staff visiting site reasonably frequently. Discussion with staff at work and off-duty can reassure site staff that their efforts are valued and their difficulties understood. Such visits help to link faces to reports and to assist understanding of the working environments to which the reports relate.

Regular, prompt, formal reports are the essential skeleton of communications between site and head office. The sophistication of the reporting system depends on the duration and complexity of the project, the availability, quality and cost of junior site staff and on the style and culture of the organisation. Progress made so far, valuations and payments, costs and cash flow are basic requirements along with a broad monitoring of labour, materials and plant costs to provide input for future estimates or tenders. Activity costing may or may not be considered appropriate and is sometimes omitted on the basis that individual projects are so different that a comparison with the tender is of historical value only, and that output ratings for purposes of future tenders are better obtained by special one-off exercises.

If the project documentation includes a project management manual it is likely to set out the form and frequency of the formal reports required. The constraints are fairly obvious, the reports have two potential values, immediate and longer term. For immediate purposes, they should contain information useful to various individuals in the head office in a form which is brief and digestible. For longer term purposes, they may be source material for any future claims or litigation and should present a coherent, continuous picture of the development of the project. The process of preparing reports should not be so burdensome as to interfere with the effective management of the project.

A further aspect of reporting arises on completion of the project, or of a major or important operation within the project. A concise, narrative completion report noting, while memory is fresh, how the operation was executed, what problems arose and their solutions, what innovations were tried and their success or failure allows the practical knowledge gained to become the company's property to be used for future projects.

Measurement and payment
This issue is crucial to the successful running of a project and, consequently, has intruded on earlier sections.

Cash flow is vital to any project to minimise cash injection or supporting overdrafts and to minimise related interest costs. In a negotiated or package proposal an attempt is usually made to allow the project to be cash positive by a small margin throughout; a degree of flexibility in interim measurement subject to subsequent refinement may be acceptable to all parties.

In a conventional tendered contract measurement is specified at fixed intervals, usually monthly, and is carried out by the contractor and verified by the client or its engineer. In practice, measurements are usually taken jointly and, with goodwill, can be taken with a cautious allowance for work in progress so that they fairly represent the work completed by the date of submission.

The valuation is prepared by the contractor and checked by the client or its engineer. These valuations are based, very largely, on existing contract rates but there will usually be items which the contractor considers are not so covered, against which additional valuations are sought. With goodwill a provisional on-account and without commitment rate or valuation can be agreed so that the valuation represents, as fairly as possible, the likely value of the work done and ultimately to be paid for. Where such agreement is not possible, the contractor receives no payment until rates are eventually fixed and cash flow suffers accordingly.

Payment is made by the client of the valuations as certified. Bureaucracy within the client's organisation may create delay, or the client may be able, if it so wishes, to influence a not wholly autonomous engineer to delay certification. In happier circumstances the contractor and the engineer have co-operated to expedite measurement, valuations and certification and the client is prepared to make payment immediately on certification, which, ideally as above, may be made on the last day of the measurement period.

Most contract conditions specify only the maximum period of delay between certification and payment; similarly, most protection provisions such as ECGD relate to default in payment after certification. The difference between consensual and confrontational site relations can have significant effect on the contractor's cash flow.

Variations and claims

Most contract documents seek to define the conditions under which instructions can be given to vary the works and the basis of payment for any such variations, as well as the conditions under which the contractor can seek additional payment in relation to work or conditions which it contends are not covered by unit rates in the BOQ or by the terms of variation orders.

As stated above, the regime of an overseas construction contract is, broadly, either consensual or confrontational.

Confrontation usually means working to the book, for the contractor this involves invoking every opportunity for a claim and for the client or its engineer resisting every such claim and requiring precise compliance with the requirements for formal notification. In some cultures claims, despite the words of the contract document, are not acceptable and a contractor who pursues a claim may have irretrievably lost a future potential client. A contractor who finds itself with such a client, and at the same time an engineer bent on confrontation is unfortunate, or should have assessed the position better in advance.

More often things go one way or the other; either all parties will accept a degree of consensus, usually with each seeking to weight matters slightly in its own favour, or both will accept that consensus cannot be reached and that the sequence of claims, rebuttals, arbitration and litigation must be pursued, to the enrichment of lawyers and the souring of any future relationship between the parties.

A contractor is usually aware of possible disadvantages from a worsening in relations consequent on notification of a contentious claim. There is said to be a hierarchy: always claim for a *force majeure*, rarely and reluctantly claim for a client's default, never claim for an engineer's default.

Where conditions of consensus prevail, one expedient solution adopted was to append to each monthly measurement a schedule of requests for additional measurement. This schedule was mutually agreed as meeting the requirement for the notification of circumstances, while avoiding both the use of the word 'claim' and any need to delay certification of the accompanying measurement. Subsequently, after unhurried consideration, some of the items scheduled were agreed as measurement, others were abandoned and, eventually, only a small residue were formally re-submitted as claims. In a major contract where this procedure was adopted, the claims submitted at final completion amounted to less than 1% of contract value and were settled for less than a quarter of 1%; the contract, incidentally, being completed to quality, ahead of time and with the contractor quietly satisfied with its profit.

Litigation

There are no immutable rules and a contractor may be faced by circumstances in which it chooses, as plaintiff, to pursue arbitration, either in the country of operation or internationally, and/or litigation either in the country of operation or in the UK, with the possible subsequent need to seek enforcement of award in the country of operation. More frequently, a contractor may find itself as defendant, resisting demands impossible to resolve amicably, from employees, suppliers or subcontractors in a local civil or shariah court, or in local arbitration.

It would be prudent for the contractor to obtain the best local advice available and representation where appropriate. This done, the contractor may be surprised and perhaps irritated by the procedure, but, surprisingly often, relieved by the fairness of the eventual award.

Part IV

Taking stock

One function of management is the taking of decisions. A convenient first stage of taking stock is to review the sequence of management decisions flowing through the preceding chapters.

Stakeholders

Such decisions have included

- o identification and acknowledgement of stakeholders
- o identification of aims of stakeholders
- o ranking of aims of stakeholders
- o identification and resolution/accommodation/elimination of hidden agendas
- o definition of aims of organisation.

Environment

Other decisions involved a three phase investigation and evaluation of aspects of the environment relevant to the current or potential operations of the organisation.

(*a*) UK: there is a need to assess, on the one hand, the ongoing comparative difficulties/advantages of operating in the UK and, on the other hand, to assess the impact of elements of the UK environment on overseas working. Factors likely to have a bearing include UK intergovernmental aid; UK government help and exhortation to UK contractors to work overseas; UK taxation, bonding, access to services and other activities of the group if any of which the contractor is part.

(*b*) The international community: relevant if the contractor is to proceed with its consideration of overseas activity. Important issues include an assessment of the current and future climate for international aid, international finance, and the prospects of international agency projects in selected regions of the world. Finally, the contractor's market intelligence can provide awareness of international competition, local participation, prevailing contract arrangements and the possibilities of international corporate acquisition of, or by, the organisation.

(*c*) The area of proposed operations: here, the elements of the environment impact on an overseas construction operation. Views need to be developed concerning the requirements of a potential client, finance and risk, political and social considerations and operating conditions in the area. Initially, the investigation and assessment of these elements is a matter of testing the water to decide whether or not to proceed further, and is appropriate to an organisation already working overseas and considering a new area. Such considerations also affect a contractor actively considering overseas projects and deciding where to go or whether to follow a specific lead.

The next and more detailed investigation and assessment overlaps the first stage of marketing and is directed towards a decision to pursue a specific area and/or a specific project; or in the case of a contractor already working overseas to withdraw from a particular area or from overseas operations generally.

Corporate management

Senior management have a responsibility to make strategic decisions about overseas working. These strategic decisions involve balancing the needs of stakeholders, assessing the input of the construction environment and making the operational decisions with the strategic objective of the firms.

The strategic considerations are constantly under review and develop. Within the generality of overseas construction they principally include

- establishing aims; what the organisation seeks to be as well as what it seeks to do
- deciding whether to work overseas. In practice many contractors flirt with the idea of working overseas and abandon the idea after a very cursory investigation. Others proceed to the first stages of marketing and if not then successful will either try again (and harder), try somewhere else, or temporarily or permanently abandon the idea of overseas working. Others, having worked overseas, decide to continue, or to try in another area, or to withdraw from overseas working. These decisions again are not forever, they are to be kept under review in relation to actual or foreseen changes in each of the elements of the environment. The comparative success or failure of the company's efforts and the perceived opportunities will shape actions.

Operation
Operation comprises marketing and performance.

The strategic decision to seek work overseas may have been made primarily in reaction to conditions in the home market, or in response to learning of an opportunity in a particular area, or in relation to a particular potential client or project. The initial decision will be to make a defined and limited marketing effort and to review proceeding further in the light of the success or failure of that effort. The key decisions at this stage are

- the choice of area and potential client. Perhaps fixed by specific opportunity, otherwise to be researched initially by head office desk study, and in either case to be evaluated by further desk study and by site visit.
- the choice between invited tender or proposal for negotiation. Again, perhaps determined by specific opportunity or in relation to specific potential client. It is likely that one potential project only would be followed in the initial venture to an area.
- the degree of establishment. Several alternatives exist. The firm can open a local office, appoint a local agent or rely on communication from the UK supported by visits. The choice of the local agent is critical as is the choice of the contractor's

representative for the first evaluation visit.

- tender sum. The price of a tender or of a proposal is a combination of estimated cost, assessed risk and commercially judged margin (positive or negative). It must reflect the organisation's belief in the market, desire to enter and, possibly, willingness to pay to do so. The submission of a tender or proposal is rarely the end of the game. Continued unremitting and well directed follow-up effort is usually essential if a contract is to be achieved.

The success or failure of any proposal or tender brings its feedback of information, complementing earlier evaluation and contributing to ongoing marketing strategy and tactics; or to a decision to abandon a particular market.

Performance covers the planning, resourcing and doing of the operation.

(a) Thorough, detailed and realistic planning is essential; it must be constantly reviewed in relation to monitored performance and any uncovenanted events, and revised as necessary.

(b) Resourcing is the selection and movement to the project site, in accordance with planning, of the human resources, equipment and materials. The choice of key individuals is of first importance, that of suitable equipment a close second.

(c) The project mandate, together with any local refining, has defined the project culture and the choice of key individuals has been the first step in implementing this. The physical establishment of the project and the development of project relationships are to follow accordingly. Motivation of all elements of the project personnel is built on this foundation and is the essential magic ingredient of performance.

Quality management and safety management are vital, must be acknowledged, are central components of the mandate and must be resourced accordingly.

Financial control, materials control, equipment maintenance, monitoring of outputs and quality, immediate and longer term record and ongoing negotiation of measurement, valuation and payment are self evidently of vital importance.

9

Epilogue

9.1. Credentials of international contracting

There is a continuing demand and need for construction in developing countries, although not all such construction is uniformly endorsed by western opinion.

Some is deemed to be unacceptably harmful to the environment. Clearly, environmental factors must be considered but it is not tenable that western opinion should put an arbitrary stop to third world development, while enjoying and seeking to enhance their own standard of living based on earlier development.

Some is held to be an uneconomic use of limited resources; there is sometimes criticism that intergovernmental aid is, by the wish of the recipient nation, applied to schemes selected on political rather than economic criteria. It should be noted, however, that such comments may be found in any country in the world. In short, a project will go ahead if the potential client wishes to proceed with the project and has, or can mobilise funds to support it. Subject to any judgement that the ethics of a particular project may be entirely unacceptable, the commercial justification is the provision of a service. Much overseas construction is directed to worthy ends; communications and industrial development, health, education and welfare. The potential client, as individual, private corporation or sovereign state is, within very wide limits, entitled to choose which project to pursue.

Against this background of demand and choice, most developing countries need a measure of external assistance, greater or lesser in the circumstances of each country, in delivering major development projects.

Such assistance, as discussed earlier, can include any or all of the following services

- concept design
- finance
- supervision
- equipment supply
- commissioning

- feasibility study
- detailed design
- construction and construction management
- operation and training.

The provision of such services is capable of abuse in seeking to promote the scheme most beneficial to the contractor, rather than that most beneficial to the client, but safeguards against this can, and should be provided in the development agreement for any major project. However, the provision of the services is not of itself exploitation and can, and should be an honourable export trade. A few UK contractors and a sufficient number of individuals are able and willing to provide such services and continue to do so and, by comparison with international standards, do so rather well.

9.2. Company and individual reasons for working overseas

These have been considered briefly in the preceding text; the individual reasons as an element of human resources motivation and the company reasons in relation to the company decision to work overseas.

For the individual there is inevitably, in considering an opportunity to work overseas, a balance of potential advantages and disadvantages in relation to the particular opportunity.[22]

The disadvantages could well include

- relative isolation
- reduced social facilities and breaking of existing social patterns
- disruption of family
- climate, health discomforts and risks
- the likelihood of longer working hours and more strenuous working conditions.

The opposing advantages could include

o higher remuneration
o the opportunity to take greater responsibility earlier than in the UK
o initially, the challenge of the relatively unknown
o travel and experience of a different environment linked recently to more generous and frequent leave patterns
o subsequently perhaps, a preference for the overseas construction life.

The balance between perceived advantages and disadvantages is obviously different for each contract and each area of work. The decisive factor is the match between this pattern and the character, circumstances and aspirations of the individual making the choice. Each individual is well advised to consider this match carefully, and to obtain as much information as possible on the project, the company culture and the local environment before accepting a first overseas appointment. Those who continue to choose and prefer working overseas find that, with a degree of selectivity of project and location, the match continues to work.

For the company there is also a balance between advantages and disadvantages. The particular choices are primarily whether or not to

• pursue a particular project opportunity; either by tender, by negotiation or by job creation
• seek work or continue to seek work in a particular overseas territory
• seek overseas work generally.

The company has considered its aims, and in relation to each such choice will consider which alternatives are more likely to contribute to the achievement of these aims. Again, there must be a match between the aims, abilities and culture of the company and the opportunities within the project and the local environment. The reasons given for a contractor choosing to work overseas usually include

• the prospect of higher profit margins commensurate with higher risk
• an option in growth diversification or to maintain workload when work is scarce in the UK.

However, it would appear that factors of company character and culture, such as the experience of its managers and senior staff of overseas construction, and related to this the company's assessment of its ability to work profitably overseas, and its managers attitude towards such work are important and are reflected in the notional balance of advantages and disadvantages above.

9.3. Requirements for success

As a simplification it is postulated that success is based on delivering an acceptable project to time and quality after first obtaining award of a contract by tender, negotiation or job creation on price terms which allow an acceptable profit margin over the costs of so performing. (It also involves doing nothing untoward during the project to dilute the client's satisfaction.)

There are, following the basic decision on working overseas, two linked and complementary but separate elements, marketing and performance. The contractor's profit being defined by its ability to secure sufficient profit margin in tendering or negotiation and by the cost effectiveness of construction performance.

This text has not aspired to be a DIY manual for contracting success; the Authors accepting the view of the contingency school that management decisions should be appropriate to circumstances. Accordingly, the text has first sought to outline the significant elements of the overall environment of a project, and then considered the appropriate positioning of the project organisation in relation to its environment. However, while acknowledging that each project is different, there are common strands of decisions and actions, but no one set of immutable rules.

Subject then to these reservations: a contractor should seek to work overseas only after deciding that to do so would further the achievement of its corporate aims. It must satisfy itself that it can market successfully and having done so can perform successfully. Successful marketing requires the identification of a target country, a target client, or a target project and a choice of market strategy in relation to tendering, negotiation or job creation. A contractor should match its market to its capabilities. Establishment of a marketing presence and the preparation and submission of a tender, or other form of offer, are costly exercises. Preliminary groundwork to establish the probability of success before incurring these costs is usually money very well spent.

Vital attributes in marketing are identification with potential clients and willingness to diversify to meet their requirements. In many cases, the trick is to compete with construction from countries with substantially lower salary costs. One way of competing is to structure an appropriate form of contractual relationship which may well differ from the traditional form and may perhaps involve a one stop shop relationship with the client.

To conclude, successful project execution requires an effective combination of

- planning and continuous monitoring of performance and progressive updating of planning
- financial control: effective mobilisation of financial resources to meet project needs and the preparation, monitoring and progressive updating of project cash flow projection and credit control
- human resources: the wise selection of senior project staff, the successful motivation of the whole project personnel and continuous contact and support
- selection: mobilisation and logistics of materials and equipment, and backup of replacement spares and services
- communications: a firm, clear mandate, of which the staff can take possession, reporting and essential continuing supportive contact between head office management and site.

Both marketing and performance depend on interpersonal relationships between the contractor and the client, or potential client, and the other organisations comprising elements of the project environment, and within the contractor's organisation.

The essential business attributes were stated[63] as 'bias for action, keeping close to the customer, nichemanship, autonomy and entrepreneurship, productivity through people, hand-on value driven leadership, quality of design, stick to the knitting, simple form lean staff, simultaneous loose tight properties with core values rigidly adhered to in a contingency structure'.

An alternative recent statement[85] gave 'analyse, keep it simple, communicate well, get on with it, re-evaluate, deter bureaucracy, fight fossilisation, innovate and learn from your mistakes'.

Not surprisingly, there is substantial common ground between either of these statements and the preceding requirements.

Part V

Case Studies

A

The Quadirabad barrage

This case study addresses several aspects of the project. All measurements are imperial.

Conversion table

1 inch	= 25·4 mm
1 foot	= 0·3048 m
1 yard	= 0·9144 m
1 (statute) mile	= 1·609 km

(a) Construction organisation and management
(b) Logistics and temporary works
(c) Construction method and innovation.

Introduction and project context

The Quadirabad barrage is a retention structure 3400 feet long across the Chenab river. The Chenab together with the Sutlej, Beas, Ravi and Jehlum are tributaries of the Indus and form the five rivers of the Punjab (Fig. 14).The site is some 60 miles from Lahore and 100 miles from Rawalpindi and Islamabad; these are the principal cities of the region.

India and Pakistan became separate independent states in 1947. The boundary under the partition agreement placed the head reaches of the southern branches of the river Indus in India. India progressively claimed these waters and the sub-

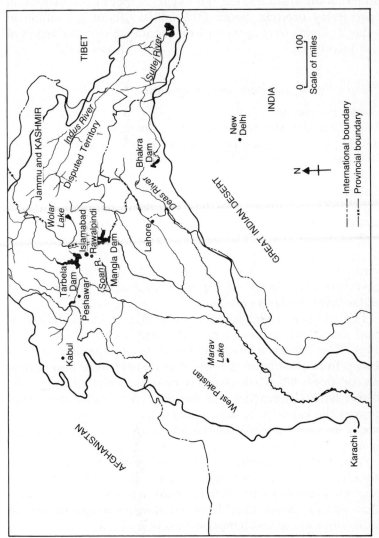

Fig. 14. Quadiraband barrage location

sequent Indus Basin Agreement, with international funding, introduced works to store and transfer water from the Indus and Jehlum to serve areas in Pakistan. The beginning of the project is an illustration of the impact of political decisions on engineering projects. Some £0·5 billion (about £4 billion in today's values) were spent on works to implement this aspect of the Agreement.

Construction organisation and management

Construction contract

The client for the works was the Government of Pakistan (GOP); acting through its agency WAPDA (Water and Power Development Authority) with American and British firms appointed under the Agreement as project consultants for design and construction. The World Bank appointed its own supervising consultants. WAPDA had their organisation at site, as well as seconding most of the staff of the project engineer's representative (ER). The supervising consultant's representative visited site regularly and all payments were required to be jointly authorised by representatives of these three parties. The payments were agreed at site level for smaller values and at higher levels for larger amounts.

The construction contracts were governed by FIDIC standard international conditions with extensive particular conditions. The contracts were awarded by competitive tenders drawn from pre-qualified contractors. These were from Pakistan or from the participating countries contributing to the World Bank. In practice, the terms for pre-qualification were beyond the capacity of most indigenous contractors, and only one of the main construction contracts was won by a Pakistani firm.

A specialist subcontractor was nominated for supply and installation of the barrage gates. The main contractor appointed specialist international contractors for ground treatment and for prestressing. Local contractors were used for the provision of camp and temporary works building.

The Quadirabad contract was awarded in 1964 with construction substantially completed in 1967. The main contractor was a consortium of Danish, French and Pakistani companies. Figure 15 illustrates the organisation structure for the project.

THE QUADIRABAD BARRAGE

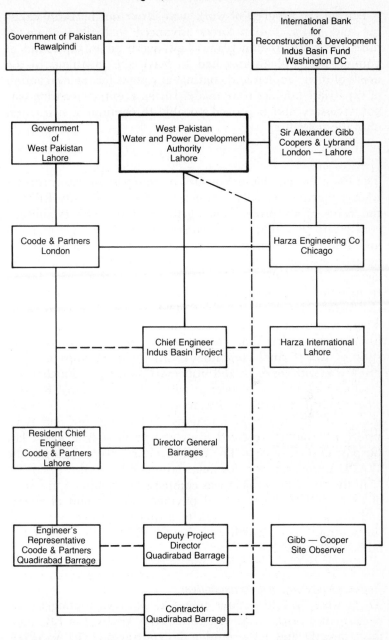

Fig. 15. Quadiraband barrage project organisation

During the progress of work, war broke out between Pakistan and India. Indian forces advanced to Sialkot, some 50 miles from site. Indian planes flew overhead to the sound of gunfire. Many Pakistanis had to leave site to attend to the needs of their families and contingency plans for the evacuation of expatriate families were made. In the event, evacuation was not necessary and it proved possible to continue construction until the cease-fire.

Communications

The main formal channel of site communication was a regular weekly meeting: usually between the ER and deputy ER and the contractor's project management team. The established convention was that the discussion could be as acrimonious and abusive as circumstances required but that only the finally agreed position should be minuted. The ER prepared the agenda, chaired the meeting, drafted the minutes, and agreed them with the project manager and the WAPDA representative before they were finalised. The system seemed to work. There was a minimum of contentious correspondence outside the meetings, other than contractually necessary formal notifications. Less formal communications included stops to chat, drink tea, with foremen and inspectors on the job. Further discussions took place over beer or whisky in the evening. Reports were submitted weekly and were aimed to be sufficiently informative to forestall most questions. Delivering any bad news before it could be received from any other source was a key purpose of such reports. The weekly minutes were copied to the WAPDA representative for information and record.

In the event the project was completed to quality and ahead of time: and the final agreed payment, on account of claims and disputed items, amounted to a quarter of one percent of the contract value, which was about £12 million, nearly £100 million in 1994 values.

Project management and administration

There were, in effect, three teams at site contributing to the performance of the contract; those of WAPDA, the ER, and, most directly and importantly, the contractor. The WAPDA representative's team consisted of members of an established department, which generally performed administrative duties for the project. The ER's staff comprised some six expatriate engineers and four trade inspectors, all British, together with Pakistani engineers and supporting office staff seconded by WAPDA. Drivers and ancillaries were provided by the contractor. The contractor's consortium was staffed by Pakistanis and 50 expatriates from eight European nations. The workforce was approximately 5000 strong, The ER's staff and contractor's staff had worked together on earlier projects. This was of great benefit for relations between and within each team and was acknowledged as contributing to the success of the project. Most of the expatriates had experience of overseas work, and most were motivated by the satisfaction gained from completing a successful project. This motivation was shared by many of the Pakistani staff and increased as the project moved towards a successful completion. There was little opportunity for team building by selection, but there was an element of weeding out and a conscious, persuasive modification of the structure of each team. The process accommodated the strengths and weaknesses of team members.

The overall planning of the works was simple with a bar chart programme monitored by output S-curves being used for the main activities. Further control was obtained by charting and forecasting each concrete pour by calendar dating.

Work was measured and paid by monthly certificate. Naturally, the contractor was concerned with cash flow and month-end figures were assembled over the last week of each month. Conservative projections for work to be completed during the week were included in the valuation. This enabled a measurement to be signed and a certificate issued immediately at the end of the month.

Logistics and temporary works

Plant, spares and material supply

The total length of the site was about ten miles and the works included creating marginal bunds (an earth bank) along the length of the works. The site was not serviced by existing roads. As work proceeded, well maintained, motorable dirt roads were built. Earlier survey and inspection trips were cross-country by Land Rover, horseback or, in emergency, camel.

The contractor's heavy equipment, principally earthmoving plant, had previously been employed on the Mailsi Syphon, some 200 miles from Quadirabad. It was too heavy to use public roads and low loaders were not available. The contractor, naturally, wished to avoid stripping down and transporting the equipment in pieces. The solution adopted was to travel cross-country. A survey party was sent out and a route found which combined shrub desert, agricultural land, and, where possible, canal maintenance paths. Supervising staff travelled with the convoy which was complete with food, drink, cooks and sleeping equipment. Their role was to organise breakdown repairs and, where necessary, make arrangements with farmers, landowners and local officials. The journey took about a week, all arrived intact.

Another major logistics issue was the movement and handling of some 600 000 tonnes of concrete aggregates, over the period of the contract. This came mainly from a quarry operated by WAPDA under a separate contract some 70 miles away. Aggregates were loaded at the quarry into rail trucks and carried over national lines to the site sidings; one spur of which served the aggregate storage and reclamation area.

Here, the contractor constructed a six foot diameter, underground pipe reclamation tunnel; it passed under stockpiles and feeders and conveyers were used to deliver aggregates directly to the central batching plant.

The isolation of the site meant that virtually nothing could be obtained quickly. Items produced in Pakistan had to travel long distances by road or rail. Imported items could, in some cases, be obtained from stockholders in Pakistan but more often they had to be imported by sea or, in the case of small items, or in an emergency, by air. Formalities such as import permits, port clearances, etc. created delays and difficulties. To these were added risks of damage or pilfering during port handling. Consequently, the contractor's site establishment included well equipped workshops to repair or replace vital components. Extensive stores held buffer stocks to bridge delivery delays.

Commercial decisions of whether to hold infrequently needed parts in stock or replace by costly air freight had to be made. In this project the delays associated with import procedures urged the contractor to carry the financial burden of holding on site as wide a range of parts and spares as possible.

As concessionary terms for the import of food and drink were granted, as part of the international funding arrangements, supply links included these items. Commissionary storage and sale facilities were provided on site.

Preliminary works

A major preliminary was land acquisition. The main river channel had moved considerably over a period of years and virtually the whole of the flood plain was cultivated between floods. Accordingly, practically the whole construction area was subject to some, past or present, rights of ownership or cultivation. There was an understandable inclination to squeeze the maximum benefit from any such rights. This factor, together with local bureaucracy and delays in payment for acquisition created a major problem of gaining access to construction areas.

WAPDA had to tackle the problem. Junior officials had surveyed the area for months and years. Contention was inevitable. There were instances (although much less than on some other sites) of farmers laying themselves and their families in the path of earthmoving equipment. They refused to move before payment was made.

The residential area, to accommodate the staff, was located some five miles from the main construction site, yet this area was still within the river flood plain. Necessarily, it was enclosed by a protective bund. WAPDA had constructed this bund, essential access roads and housing for supervising staff under separate earlier contracts.

On award of the main contract, the contractor built (also within the bunded area) accommodation for his own, and subcontractor employees. The compound included a well equipped project hospital, club with bar, swimming pool and squash court for the use of the senior staff. The definition of 'senior' was tactfully drawn to include all expatriates. A school was built, which taught 60 children at its peak. The children were drawn from twelve nationalities and were all taught in English. Conversation outside the classroom was happily in an amalgam of their different languages.

As an additional amenity, it was found that the heavy plant could mould a borrow pit area into a nine hole golf course. This was incredibly rough, with sand 'browns', but was greatly appreciated, if only for an early morning hour before the site office opened at 7 o'clock.

Other preliminary works performed by the contractor were a temporary power station to supply camp and works, a road spur, rail spur and sidings.

The installation of the railway created an interesting situation. At that time, the Railway Department manuals had been successively copied without major revision since before independence. In the process a vital square root sign had become misplaced and, in issuing the information, the ER failed to spot this as did the contractor's engineer. When the first truck took to the railway a crossfall of some six times what it should have been was evident.

The decision not to submit a claim, on account of wrongful information, is a comment upon the quality of relations on site at that time. The contractor's site manager had noted at the start of the project that co-operation rather than conflict was to be the credo of the contract. This philosophy greatly assisted the progress of the works.

However, the dominant issue of the preliminary works was the seasonal flooding in the Chenab. The flood season is reasonably well defined, but there is virtually no advance warning of the magnitude of the flood in any one year. Accordingly, projects such as this must be prepared each year for a predicted maximum flood; that, for the Chenab, being approximately 1 000 000 cusecs.

The permanent works design normally incorporates massive armoured guide banks to direct flood flows during operation. Figure 16 shows the layout of the guide banks. The classic construction procedure, as used on the Nile barrages, is to build outwards from one bank during one dry season, then to batten down. This allows the river to pass over, and through, completed work. Immediately the flood abates work begins from the other bank in the hope of closing safely before the next year's flood arrives. It is a procedure which often succeeded, but sometimes did not; and one which demands good logistics and good nerves. Quadirabad was planned on this basis at the design stage. However, in the preceding Mailsi project the contractor had engaged as a consultant, Sir Thomas Foy, an eminent member of the pre war Indian Irrigation Service. He produced an alternative, which proved successful, and which was now repeated at Quadirabad. The Chenab at low flow was directed into a pilot channel; 17–20 feet wide and 3–4 feet deep through sand silt deposits of the river bed near the western bank.

It is worth noting that the vehicle crossing, over the dry weather flow, was made of some ten, 40 gallon oil drums, side by side, covered with sand, and that the entire dry weather flow passed comfortably through these pipes. As the river began to rise, the crossing was hastily removed so increasing flows through the channel. This flow scoured the bed and banks thereby enlarging the channel, and for much of the initial rise the entire flow was contained in and carried by the new channel. Inevitably, as the river continued to rise the banks were over-topped, but by this time the main flow of the river remained centred on the new alignment, keeping its main erosive power away from the work area.

Meanwhile dewatering and excavation of the main barrage area had continued, the spoil forming the permanent guide banks.

Construction method and innovation

The earthworks

Quadirabad barrage (Fig. 17), designed by British consultants, was the latest in a developing family of water retaining structures built on permeable foundations. In the evolution of design, earlier attempts had eventually failed due to water scouring away the foundation material and so undermining the structure. Turbulent flow created at the toe of the structure had a similar effect. Progressively the foundation was extended to avoid these failures. Then, in the interest of economy, sheet piles were introduced to deepen the under structure flow path. Flow nets were drawn, exit gradients calculated, and downstream aprons thickened and sloped to resist upward pressure and dissipate energy.

The working area, contained within a ring of earth banks in the flood plain, required excavation substantially below the dry weather river bed level. This factor, coupled with decisions to work continuously through the wet seasons, raised the scale of dewatering necessary (dewatering discharge to the river downstream was in total 4500 million cubic feet). This was achieved

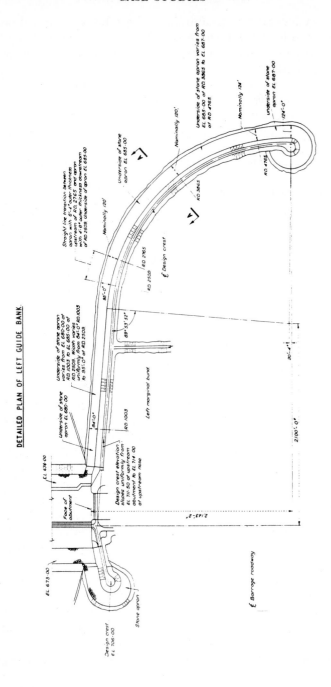

DETAILED PLAN OF LEFT GUIDE BANK.

162

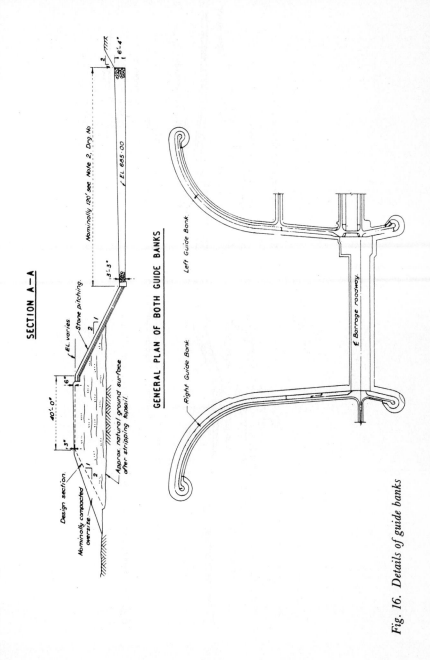

Fig. 16. Details of guide banks

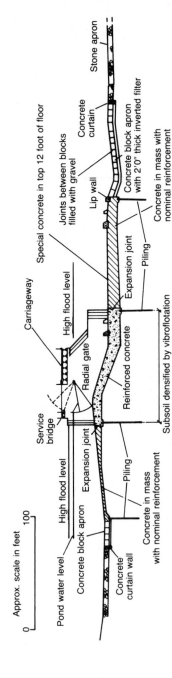

Fig. 17. Typical cross-section through the main barrage structure

by a complete ring of deep wells surrounding the site, with the concentration of pumps moved from one end to the other as construction progressed. This worked, with only minimal supplementary wellpointing.

This technique had two beneficial by-products: the ready availability of water allowed spray curing of concrete and the control of groundwater levels proved a major element in ground densification.

The major earthworks were performed by teams of dozer assisted motor scrapers; compaction by smooth wheeled, vibrating rollers complemented by heavy, high speed rubber tyred tractors. Moisture content for compaction was achieved by advance flooding of borrow pits and adequate bowser capacity at the point of placing.

The contractor's plant management was crucial. Careful selection and balancing of plant was critical to earthworks' performance. Further, the location of borrow pits influenced the progress of works. A full maintenance and spares organisation was necessary to keep the fleet mobile.

The design of the barrage required the improvement of the underlying foundation. The ground consolidation was based on the Cementation Vibrofloation system. The contractor, after considering alternatives, engaged Cementation UK as subcontractor. The level of consolidation achieved was tested by hand boring and sampling to measure densities after treatment. In a sudden moment of revelation, the contractor realised that the densities achieved in the earthworks were higher than those required for ground consolidation. Costs could be reduced by excavating, replacing and compacting the earth which had been made workable by the dewatering system. The ER was enthusiastic, but needed higher approval. He was technically satisfied that the scheme would work and asked for the scheme to be approved suggesting a consequent reduction in contract value.

Approval was granted together with an instruction that a price reduction was unnecessary since there was no reduction in the quality of the work!

The concrete work
The production of concrete, 440 000 cubic yards in total, was central to the project. The contractor's aggregate storage and

reclamation arrangements provided a reliable and continuous supply of crushed stone to the central batching plant. These stone aggregates were adequately hard and strong but were poorly shaped, giving a mix highly susceptible to variable water content. This, together with the high temperatures during transportation and placing, led to the extensive use of plasticising agent in the mixes.

The quality of stone became an issue on the project. Good stone would lead to good concrete. The unofficial story circulating was that an eminent international expert was consulted to select the source of the stone. Due to other commitments he agreed to undertake a desk study and an aerial survey. The recommendation of the source of stone was qualified by a note that a field investigation should be undertaken to support his

Fig. 18. Concrete placement

conclusions. However, the eminence of the expert overcame any reservations that more fully informed local authorities may have had, and his selection was endorsed.

All concrete was placed by crane, using bottom opening buckets (Fig. 18). Delivery to the placing point was by flat-bed trucks, each able to hold one full and one empty bucket. On each trip every truck ran under the batching plant, to allow an empty bucket to be filled. This was then carried to the placing crane, which released its empty bucket from the previous delivery on to the truck before picking up the full bucket for placing. This method allowed the truck to return to the batcher and repeat the cycle.

The river gates

Besides supporting the gates, the piers carried a roadway designed for full military loading. The bridge beams, precast and post-tensioned, were made, cured and stored in an area adjoining the batching plant. When required they were hauled to site on a purpose built trailer, lifted and manoeuvred into position by two mobile cranes.

The main radial gates of the barrage were provided, under nominated subcontract, by a Japanese company. Golf on the rough hewn course was so popular with the gate erection crew that on occasion the contractor had to remind the subcontractor that gates, rather than golf, were the main purpose of the exercise. Following this clarification the subcontractor performed splendidly.

There were three successive subcontracts for gates in three successive barrages of the Indus project. The first, comprising vertical lift gates (secured successfully to the piers by Araldite in spite of many fears) was won by a British company; the second by a Japanese firm; and the third was won by a Pakistani company. This seems to be fair example of technology transfer. The configuration of the gates (Fig. 19) and other parts of the construction (Fig. 20) are illustrated.

Other construction features

The downstream element of the structure consisted of massive blocks, as flexible apron, designed to have a 2 inch gravel filled

Fig. 19. Gate configuration

space between each block. Rather than precast and position each block the contractor commissioned demountable, steel shutters allowing the in situ casting of the blocks. The shutters were capable of being removed from the space between blocks for repeated re-use.

Sheet piles in the cut-off membranes, and elsewhere, were pitched by crane, retained in position by hand-held guy ropes and driven by double acting pneumatic hammers. To align the piles a worker was lifted by crane to sit, unsupported, on a small pad astride already pitched piles, marrying the clutches, as each successive pile, hanging freely from a crane was lifted into position. Health and safety were less than rigidly enforced, but fortunately there were no serious accidents.

The permanent guide banks shown in Fig. 16 were protected at the toe by flexible dumped stone aprons and on their slopes by hand placed stone pitching. This stone consisted of inter-locking handworked stones, 20 inches deep, on a graded stone filter bed. The temporary protective spurs were of similar con-struction but less rigid specification. The laying of such pit-ching was a traditional skill and its exponents (Fig. 22) were almost all Pathans from the northern regions of the country. As a matter of tribal culture, these gentlemen rarely moved out of

Fig. 20. Quadirabad barrage construction: (top) stone pitching and filter layers and (above) piers awaiting bridge beams

reach of their rifle and full bandolier, and were clearly ready and practised in their use. The inspectors were required not to be influenced by this in accepting or rejecting a man's day's work!

Fig. 21. Barrage from upstream

Summary

The project had a political background and was internationally financed. Its organisation necessarily reflected this.

The management structure and style of the different site teams and the site communications arrangements were designed to be appropriate and responsive to project conditions and its environment.

The considerable difficulties of logistics arose from the location of the site and conditions in the country at that time.

The principal innovations, i.e., the river diversion, the ground densification and the in situ casting of apron blocks, all worked satisfactorily.

The project was a success because it was planned and performed by a good team, who had experience in that type of work and were confident of their ability to repeat earlier success. They were well equipped and supported, and wanted the satisfaction of a job well done.

Finally, good relations between the parties on site contributed to project success.

Fig. 22. (Top) downstream block apron and (above) surface of stone pitching

B

Jebal Ali harbour excavation

This case study covers the main aspects of the project

(*a*) The creation and negotiation of the project
(*b*) Project organisation, mobilisation and logistics
(*c*) Preliminary and permanent works.

Jebal Ali harbour and industrial area is located some 35 kilo-metres from Dubai, in the United Arab Emirates. It is situated between Dubai and Abu Dhabi. A location plan is shown in Fig. 23.

The project is one of a series of development projects for which the then ruler of Dubai, Sheikh Rashid, was the driving force. The projects which were promoted included in addition to roads and airports, hospitals of international standing, low cost housing and other social facilities.

The creation and negotiation of the project

In 1968 Dubai was still a small trading community based on Dubai Creek and cross-Gulf traffic. It was little affected by the oil boom beginning in Abu Dhabi. Among the contractors operating in the region was Pauling Plc, who began operating in Abu Dhabi in 1964 and established a joint company with a transport organisation in Dubai in 1974.

This joint company, initially Pauling–Dutco later Dutco–Pauling, was effectively the beginning of the Dutco group. The

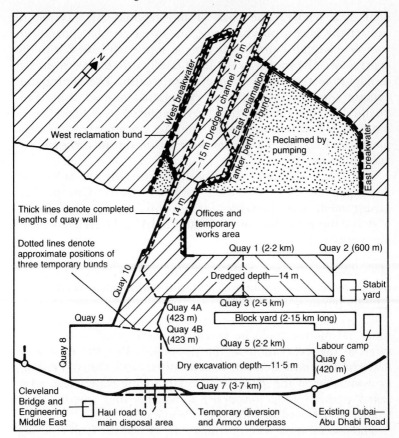

Fig. 23. Traditional pitch-laying

group grew to contain joint companies with Costain and Blankervoort (Gulf Cobla) and Balfour Beatty and Stevin (Mina Jebal Ali Construction (MJAC)).

By 1977 local participation in construction was essentially through a number of family groups. Each group, of which Dutco was one, was based on a local family and included one or more international firm. Many of the Dubai development project contracts were awarded to one or other of these groups on the basis of the ruler's instruction to negotiate a contract price with his UK consultants. Sometimes this negotiation was based upon a submitted tender, at other times it was independent of a tender. The basis of the negotiations was not to extract the lowest possible price but to ensure the capacity to complete a quality project on time at a price at least fair to the contractor. The profits to the local family group were regarded as a part of the distribution of state wealth. The contractual climate was, similarly, one of exceptional mutual trust. Frequently smaller roads, which were required in a hurry, were more than half finished before contract documents were completed and signed. Payments were made on an advance on-account basis.

The Jebal Ali project had been initiated by the ruler and developed by his consultants and the Dutco Group. The arrangement was formalised as a contract with Gulf Cobla undertaking the dredging works and MJAC, the civil engineering works.

At this stage the whole of the berth walls were designed and planned to be formed in short lengths in excavated, dewatered trench, with the dumpling of material within each basin subsequently removed by dredging.

Somewhere along the line, someone had the idea that both time and money could be saved if it were possible to execute some of the excavation in the dry and utilise the excavated material for controlled fill. Shortly afterwards Dutco–Pauling, as a member of the group with earthmoving experience, were asked whether they considered it possible and whether they would be prepared to undertake the work.

The crucial issue was, of course, the risk of the Gulf entering the excavation during the operation. The nearest point of the intended dry excavation, as Fig. 23 shows, was 2000 metres from the original coastline but, with the intention that as dry excavation and dredging both proceeded, this could be reduced to about 110 metres.

Pauling's engineering director was asked to fly out immediately to assess the position. Fortunately, his experience included two barrage projects on the Sutlej and Jehlum rivers in the Indus Basin in Pakistan. These involved major excavations within earth embankments wholly surrounded by rivers in flood, the excavations being maintained dry by a ring of deep well pumps discharging to a collecting ring main. There was some similarity between the Dubai Beach Sands and the Indus Valley Sands and it was decided to advise Pauling that dry excavation would be possible. An amicable redistribution of the work was arranged with Dutco–Pauling becoming a nominated subcontractor to Gulf Cobla. The subcontract involved dewatering the area and all risks of water entry were subsumed under the subcontract. The excavation totalled 33 million cubic metres of material leaving a hole four kilometres long, with a maximum width of 800 metres and depths between 9–14 metres, included underlying hard material and controlled disposal and compaction of excavated material in a nearby reclamation area. Payment was a negotiated rate per cubic metre to be agreed with the ruler's consultants who were the Dubai offshoot of Halcrow of the UK. This can be considered as an application of value engineering made possible by the early involvement of the contractor in the project development process. The contract was possible because of access to other resources within the contractor's group. The benefits it offered and delivered included

- a reduction in dredging requirement at a time of other calls on group resources
- the ability to construct approximately half of the total length of quay wall in the dry with unrestricted working access
- improved control of reclamation filling together with earlier completion and a substantial saving in cost to the client.

Project organisation, mobilisation and logistics

This subcontract was, inevitably, the last major element of the project to be negotiated and the first required to be complete. There was naturally some sense of urgency.

The agreement was quickly formalised as a subcontract, unusually simple in that virtually all risks were borne by the subcontractor and virtually all payments covered by one item of dig, haul, place and compact. Terms of payment included an advance payment related to the need for plant purchase and repayable in instalments from certified measurement payments. Although the formal contract structure was a subcontract a high degree of autonomy was experienced and for all practical purposes the contract was a full direct contractor relationship with the consultant. Two factors enabled this situation: firstly, the Dutco–Pauling organisation had enjoyed previous good relationships with the consultants; secondly, the contract was largely technically independent of other work packages.

Site relations

Halcrow International, Dubai had been established for some years and had an established office and continuing operation in Dubai. They were retained directly by the ruler's office independently of Halcrow, London who, however, seconded management and staff and provided such other assistance and services as were required.

Dutco–Pauling, although established only three years earlier, also had an ongoing Dubai establishment and had a working relationship with Halcrow from previous work in the Middle East. The working relationships were informal and flexible; the relatively short distance between Dubai and Jebal Ali allowed staff from either Dubai office to participate in site meetings whenever necessary.

The project structure within Dutco–Pauling was similarly informal and flexible. Under the company agreement, Pauling provided all technical management and a general manager seconded to Dutco–Pauling who reported to Pauling's managing director. In practice he maintained a close relationship with the local partner, ensuring that he was fully informed of all developments and sought his advice on all matters with local commercial or political implications. He soon learnt when such advice should be treated as though it were an instruction.

At departmental level Pauling always operated a matrix structure. The formal line of command was Managing Director (London)—General Manager (Dubai)—Project Manager (Jebal Ali), but this was supplemented by the head of each department in London also dealing directly with the corresponding head of their specialisation both in Dubai and in Jebal Ali. Such a system clearly offers risk of crossed wires and to reduce such risk the company deliberately sought to strengthen personal relationships; frequent visits by senior London staff to site, where they could renew contacts and appreciate the conditions under which site staff were working, were encouraged. Site staff called in at the London office during leave and were taken for a drink or for lunch.

During the period 1975–1985 Pauling maintained an

average annual work turnover of approximately £140 million in 1994 values, wholly overseas and with a London office strength never more than 100. The organisation was characterised by informality and flexibility. Senior staff acknowledged their own limitations and relied on their colleagues' strengths; when mistakes were made they were admitted and remedied.

This was made easier by the size of the organisation in which each of the three executive directors worked regularly with a substantial section of the staff and knew all of them and could be approached by any of them. The flexibility allowed by these arrangements was held to be valuable; any director could act for either of the others if necessary. It was said that if a commercial opportunity demanded an immediate answer that answer had to be 'no', but that a considered response could usually be given within 24 hours, allowing time for discussion by phone and for sleeping on it.

Project resources
Key staff for the project could be transferred immediately from the ongoing Dubai operations and temporary works started, but considerable recruitment had to be done to assemble the skills necessary to complete the project.

The first and most crucial item was dewatering. Contacts within the company led to Imperial College, London who nominated Dr Mike de Freitas to inspect the site and apply his expertise to assessing the nature and location of the limestone breccia formed from the hills parallel to the coast. Further, he was commissioned to assess the overlying beach sand and the foreseeable inflow of water through these materials to the excavation. His advice, fully justified in the event, was to confirm that dewatering was feasible by a wellpoint system and that this was more economical than deep wells.

Next, came the basic decision on dig and haul. The immediate similarity of the proposed operation to opencast mining led to hasty visits to sites in the North of England, South Wales and Germany. The obvious efficiency of the German operation stimulated consideration of a combination of large, bucket wheeled excavators and transfer and distribution conveyers. However, factors of cost effectiveness and the long lead time for equipment delivery when measured against a short contract period, swayed the decision to shovels and dump trucks. The implementation of these decisions was crucial.

Proposals, including price, for wellpoint systems were invited from Sykes and Millers, the two major UK specialists at the time, and on the basis of these proposals Millers were chosen. For the truck and shovel operation, a 4–5 kilometre haul distance led to the selection of 50-ton dump trucks with price, delivery and after sales support dictating the choice of Euclid units from the UK. For shovels, similar factors led to choice of O&K RH75 units from Germany with 7·5 cubic metre face shovel buckets or 5·5 cubic metre backhoe buckets. Since these excavators were to hold so crucial a role in performance, a small, London based, Anglo-German specialist service consultancy, Gulf Transac, were engaged to keep a specialist eye on the arrangements for the initial supply and delivery of spares.

With the construction plant being the key resource the company relied heavily on its group plant manager. Financial factors which needed to be considered were ownership costs to the contract and the operating costs. Equally important was whether each piece of equipment could deliver the required output, its reliability and ease and frequency of maintenance.

A balance between these factors had to be made, taking into account the knock-on effect of one piece of equipment being unable to work if another was broken down. Decisions were made quickly.

The ordering and forwarding to site of equipment and necessary spares was a major operation; orders for equipment were placed following negotiation with suppliers of favourable prices and support packages. All major plant and materials for Jebal Ali arrived through the recently completed facilities of Port Rashid in Dubai. Dutco-Pauling provided their own craneage, low loaders and a service truck with fuel, oil and water for equipment arriving by ro-ro vessels.

Dutco-Pauling had an established office, stores, workshops and staff camp in Dubai but the considerable expansion of workload of this project demanded additional facilities and substantial stores and workshops which were provided at Jebal Ali. The throughput of spares and their vital part in the efficiency of the operation led to the air-conditioning of the main covered stores and the installation of a fully computerised stores control system for the first time in the Pauling Group operations. The additional workforce for the contract was almost wholly recruited through labour agencies in India, Pakistan and Sri Lanka. Dutco-Pauling's staff travelled to Karachi, Bombay and Colombo to select the labour. Engagement and immigration formalities followed, with air passage to Dubai in itself a significant problem in logistics. A further minor problem was transport around the site and this was solved by the purchase and freighting to Dubai of retired double-decker London buses. These were repainted in their original scarlet and prominently displayed when the Jebal Ali Harbour was formally opened by the Queen and the Duke of Edinburgh.

However, the major site logistics issue was the carrying of excavated material across the Dubai–Abu Dhabi highway to placing areas. The frequency of the necessary dump truck crossings, together with the quantity of traffic and style of driving, constituted a problem only satisfactorily solvable by a separated level crossing. To provide this within the time available a nest of four Armco steel tubes, each 9 metres wide, 8 metres high and 130 metres long, was provided. A system of electronically controlled lights for traffic through the culverts was designed and installed but its use was quietly discontinued and control maintained by flagmen to general satisfaction and without significant accident.

Preliminary and permanent works

Dutco–Pauling peak site strength on the project included some 120 UK expatriates including excavator operators and fitters. These staff were supported by 1400 contract immigrants. The temporary works included married accommodation for a few senior staff and bachelor accommodation for all other employees. The only social or recreational facilities provided for expatriates at Jebal Ali were a bar in the mess, television and video. The established facilities included stores and workshops as well as the usual site offices. By this time, Dubai had a wide range of hotels and restaurants, there were excellent hospital facilities, privately run schools and a range of sporting activities if any time could be found to participate.

The main items of the project plant list were

- o seven O&K RH75 excavators
- o two Anderson Mavour E10 bucketwheel excavators

○ two NCK 605 dragline excavators
○ twenty-four Terex TS24 scrapers
○ sixty Euclid R50 dump trucks.

The temporary works provisions for equipment included the air-conditioned computer controlled stores. These stores supplied workshops which included track and tyre shops and machine shops for equipment assembly on arrival and for preventive and breakdown maintenance during the project.

Road access to the Jebal Ali area was provided by the Abu Dhabi–Dubai highway. Roundabout offtakes from this highway to serve the port area were installed progressively during the harbour contract and constructed by Dutco–Pauling under smaller, concurrent contracts.

The overall concept of the Jebal Ali development included use of the spoil from the harbour excavation in controlled filling to provide suitable areas for subsequent construction in the industrial development. The area initially designated to receive the total fill from the dry excavation was situated at a distance of 4–5 kilometres and on the other side of the Abu Dhabi–Dubai highway.

The Armco culvert sections were provided by Armco and their representative supervised erection with supporting fill placed and compacted as erection proceeded alongside the highway, which was then diverted over the culverts to allow free passage from the site to the disposal area.

Dewatering

The ruling decision on dewatering was the adoption of well-pointing and the choice of Millers as specialist contractor. The planning was based on dividing the operation into two stages. Firstly, wellpointing was provided to enable excavation through the overlying sand. Open grips and sumps were dug as a second phase to drain the underlying breccia. The excavation was divided into two sections to give staggered access to subsequent wall construction with separating bunds to be breached after completion of the excavation. The construction method was developed in meetings between Pauling, Dr de Freitas and Miller. Dr de Freitas estimated the water discharge and Millers made their recommendations for the installation of dewatering equipment. Pauling chose to apply a factor of safety and ordered 44 pumps each with a rated capacity of 60 l/s.

The length of header pipes and discharge pipeline of the wellpoint system were each in excess of 1 km. A system of piezometers was installed and read regularly in order to provide some advance warning if a change in groundwater conditions should develop. These instruments would indicate if a serious flow of water to the excavation was imminent. Fortunately, maximum wellpoint discharge was 380 l/s, very close to the lower limit of the Dr de Freitas' prediction and well within the pumping capacity provided.

Blasting accounted for some 14·8 million cubic metres of excavated material and, in addition, some 4·4 million cubic metres of breccia were excavated without blasting. The initial intention was to blast only material too hard to dig without blasting but excessive wear on excavators and the irregularity of the formation made this uneconomic. Therefore, all breccia was blasted with some attempt to modify the drilling pattern and hole charging to suit different hardness in the rock. Some 2·3 million linear metres of hole were drilled by a team of eight, Atlas Copco Roc crawler rigs and two, Damco rigs with portable compressors; blasting was carried out between shifts during the hot period in the middle of the day.

Early in the project the designation of an additional spoil area allowed a significant part of the overlying sand to be dumped much closer to the point of excavation. This new spoil area allowed the contractor's existing scraper fleet to contribute to the operation. The change shortened the project duration.

Managerial action was focused upon the performance of the main items of equipment, these should, as far as possible, be able to work continuously at their maximum outputs. For the scrapers, that meant that enough dozers should be available in the right place to ensure that they were promptly and quickly push loaded. For the bucketwheels and RH75s, that dump trucks should be available in the right place to receive excavated material. In addition, for the RH75s, that sufficient D9s should be available to push loose blasted material into convenient position for loading. It was essential that the bottom of the excavation should be kept as smooth as possible to enable easy access for the vehicles. Haul roads were well maintained and preventive maintenance was carried out regularly and reliably, and breakdown maintenance efficiently and promptly.

Table 2 shows reported average outputs over the duration of the contract for each type of equipment, but it must be noted that this manifestly does not compare like with like since the RH75s were generally loading large, hard, rough blasted material.

A fleet of dozers were divided between the excavation, where mainly CAT D9s cleared the bottom and heaped up loose material for loading, and the disposal areas, where mainly D8s rough levelled and distributed the dumped spoil.

Two graphs showing the performance of the digging and hauling of the sand overlay are shown in Figs 24 and 25.

These figures showing variations in operating costs, need to be viewed with caution. The charging of depreciation is subject to individual company policies and the inclusion of such items as general site bulldozing in the excavation item are matters for individual costing systems and, accordingly, they have been omitted from the cost analysis. However, the general picture is clear; the costs related to the different excavating units other than scrapers are closely comparable; the bucketwheel is the cheapest but its flexibility is least. The scraper is shown to be competitive only at very short hauls, although scrapers have talents which find a place for them in most plant fleets and are often used significantly beyond the indicated economic limit of haul distance.

Table 2. Average outputs over contract period

	Average output: m^3	
Equipment	Per machine shift hour	Per machine working hour
Seven RH75 excavators	292	375
Two bucketwheel excavators	135	200
Two draglines	101	133
Up to 24 TS24 scrapers	49	84

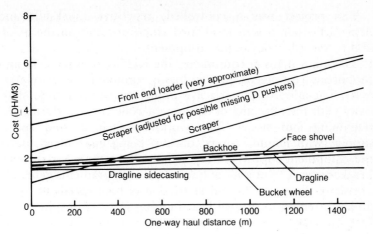

Fig. 24. Variation of operating cost (excluding depreciation) with the one-way haul distance

As noted, the quality and condition of haul roads were vital to satisfactory plant operation and these were formed with selected excavated material, and regularly and conscientiously watered and graded. Graders also provided the finer levelling of dumped spoil in acceptable layers for compaction to specified density by mixed teams of rollers.

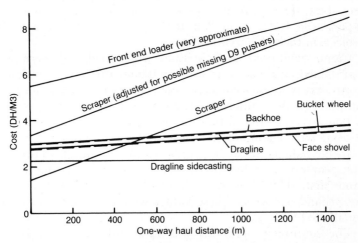

Fig. 25. Variation of operating cost (including depreciation) with the one-way haul distance

The project was a controlled, repetitive muckshift and depended upon a well motivated workforce and on the availability and efficiency of the equipment.

The main items of equipment, the RH75s, dump trucks and supporting equipment, proved highly suitable for their relative tasks. The adopted pattern of working was two, ten hour shifts daily with the servicing of equipment concentrated during the remaining four hours. The workshop facilities and spares supply (with manufacturers' backup being guaranteed under the equipment supply package) limited the time lost through breakdowns. The quality of haul roads with gradients generally not more than 1 in 30 and restriction of haul speeds to below 50 km/h served to control heat buildup in tyres in spite of the high ambient temperatures. Over the period of the excavation the dump trucks only required a second set of tyres. This was significantly less than the planned allowance and, since each tyre cost about £3000 at 1994 current values, this was a significant saving. The other main factor in the project's success was the workforce.

The operators of the RH75s were highly trained and experienced British expatriates. They enjoyed the most favourable working conditions on site with well designed cabins, good visibility, comfortable seats and air-conditioning. Such conditions were provided to ensure that the operators were able to give of their best. The remainder of the plant fleet was manned by experienced Indian and Pakistani operators trained on major projects in their home countries.

Camp conditions and facilities were good; all were well maintained and managed and the labour turnover was significantly less than for some other contractors in the Middle East. All were, by their differing standards, well paid with a prospect of bonus payments. All had the satisfaction as work proceeded of being part of a manifestly successful operation.

In the balance between people orientation and task orientation people were deliberately well looked after but the project came first. This was the culture of the operation and was known and accepted. These values were also known to apply equally to senior staff.

The contract programme was 42 months duration. It was essential that this was met despite the potential problems.

Early on the project management effort was directed to

buildup output to meet requirements, after that the site developed its own momentum; improvements and short cuts were devised and introduced. Individually each innovation was small but each contributed both to progress and to morale.

In the event, excavation was completed in 24 months, an average production of over 1·3 million m³ per month.

Summary

The project was by any standard a major earthmoving operation.

The initiation of the project was peculiar to Dubai at that particular time. It achieved its purpose and all major parties were satisfied.

The change from dredging to dry excavation for this part of the work gave an overall saving in both time and money.

The major technical decision was the feasibility of the dry excavation. Fortunately, this decision was right. Subsequent second order decisions were the method of dewatering, the temporary culvert road crossing, and the method of dig and haul. This last was a close decision at the time. The later changes in disposal requirements would have been much more difficult to accommodate if the alternative of large bucketwheel and conveyer had been chosen. There may be a moral there; construction is an uncertain world and flexibility may pay.

The selection of plant; its expeditious procurement and forwarding, together with the arrangements for spares and for preventive and breakdown maintenance were important.

The quality, motivation and performance of the entire workforce was good, based on carefully selected transfer from ongoing Dutco–Pauling operations in Dubai, considerably supplemented by recruitment in India, Pakistan and Sri Lanka, as well as the UK. Labour turnover compared very favourably with that of other contractors in the area.

The flexible and largely informal structure, and the company and project culture seem to have been appropriate to the project and to have contributed to success.

It was a muckshifting contract, nothing was particularly clever; it was performed profitably and well ahead of time. Moreover, the construction method chosen gave a significant financial saving to the client.

A recipe for business success noted in the text is: analyse, keep it simple, communicate well, get on with it, re-evaluate, deter bureaucracy, fight fossilisation, innovate and learn from your mistakes. A number of these ingredients seem to have been present in Jebal Ali.

References

1. BURTON A. *The railway empire.* John Murray, London, 1994.
2. BON R. Whither global construction? *Part 1. Building Research and Information*, 1994, **22**, No. 2.
3. BON R. The future of international construction. *Habitat International*, 1992, **16**, No. 3.
4. WORLD BANK. *The construction industry—issues and strategies in developing countries.* Washington, 1986.
5. CARRILLO P. Technology transfer in construction. *Organisation and management of construction.* CIB W65 Symposium, Trinidad, 1993.
6. KUMARASWAMY M. M. Growth strategies for less developed construction industries. *Proc. ARCOM Conf.* Loughborough, 1994.
7. HARVEY R. and ASHWORTH A. *The construction industry of Great Britain.* Butterworth-Heinemann, Oxford, 1993.
8. FLANAGAN R. The features of successful construction companies in the international construction market. *Strategic Planning in Construction Conf.* Haifa, 1994.
9. NEWCOMBE R. *et al. Construction management, Vol. 1.* Batsford, London, 1990.
10. LANGFORD D. A. and MALE S. *Strategic management in construction.* Gower, 1991.
11. HILLEBRANDT P. M. *Analysis of the British construction industry.* Macmillan, London, 1984.
12. COX V. L. *International construction—marketing, planning and execution.* Construction Press, 1983.
13. CHANNON D. F. *Cranfield Institute of Technology Case.* Trafalgar House, Cranfield, Beds, 1980.
14. CAMPBELL A. *London Business School Case.* Tarmac plc, Cranfield, Beds, 1986.

15. HAMMAM N. N. Multinational working: the challenge of work overseas. In (BURGESS R. (ed.).) *Management in the construction industry.* Mitchell, London, 1988.
16. LOVEDAY A. W. Aspects of carrying out work overseas by contract: the viewpoint of the contractor. *ICE Civil engineering problems overseas,* London, 1958.
17. CROMER EARL OF. *Export business from capital projects overseas.* HMSO, London, 1968.
18. CHANNON D. F. *The service industries: strategy, structure and financial performance.* Macmillan, London, 1978.
19. HILLEBRANDT P. M. *Economic theory of the construction industry.* Macmillan, London, 1985.
20. HILLEBRANDT P. M. The management of large UK contracting firms—theory and practice. In (LANSLEY P. and HARLOW P. E. (eds.).) *Management construction worldwide.* Spon, London, 1987.
21. MORRIS D. *The economic system in the UK.* Oxford University Press, 1985.
22. STASSMAN W. and WELLS J. *The global construction industry, strategies for entry, growth and survival.* Unwin Hyman, London, 1988.
23. ENDWICK P. Multinational contracting in the multinational service firm. In (ENDWICK P. (ed.).) *The multinational services* from Ronhedge, 1989.
24. ENSHASSI A. and BURGESS R. Training for construction site managers involved with multinational work teams. *Intl. J. of Project Management,* 1990, **8**, No. 2.
25. CENTRAL STATISTICAL OFFICE AND *THE ECONOMIST. One hundred years of economic statistics.*
26. HOBBS G. D. Long waves of economic activity. In (MORRIS D. (ed.).) *The economic system in the UK.* Oxford University Press, 1990.
27. MATHEWS *et al. British economic growth 1856–1973.* Clarendon, Oxford, 1982.
28. BARNETT C. Long term industrial performance in the UK. The role of education and research, 1850–1939. In (MORRIS D. (ed.).) *The economic system in the UK.* Oxford University Press, 1985.
29. DEPARTMENT OF EMPLOYMENT. *Housing and construction statistics.* HMSO, 1991.
30. LANSLEY P. Corporate strategy and survival in the UK construction industry. *Construction Management and Economics,* 1987, **5**.
31. BALL M. *Rebuilding construction, economic changes in the construction industry,* Routledge, London, 1988.

REFERENCES

32. NEWCOMBE R. *Construction practice workbook MP3*. University of Bath, 1991.
33. EXPORT GROUP FOR THE CONSTRUCTION INDUSTRIES. *Annual reports*. HMSO, London, 1991.
34. SEYMOUR H. D. *The multinational construction industry*. Croome Helm, London, 1987.
35. LIMERICK EARL OF. Selling construction abroad. In (URRY S. and SHERRATT A. (eds.).) *International construction*. Construction Press, Lancaster, 1980.
36. IMBERT I. D. International construction and developing countries. In (LANSLEY P. and HARLOW P. E. (eds.).) *Managing construction worldwide*. Spon, London, 1987.
37. MALE S. Competitive advantage in the international construction industry. In (MALE S. and STOCKS R. (eds.).) *Competitive advantage in construction*. Butterworth, London, 1991.
38. INTERNATIONAL BANK FOR RECONSTRUCTION AND DEVELOPMENT. *The construction industry, issues and strategies in developing countries*. Washington, 1984.
39. PARRISH A. R. The changing role of consultants. *ICE Management of Construction Projects*. London, 1984.
40. SIMON VISCOUNT. *Civil engineering problems overseas*. ICE, London, 1953.
41. CHALIBI A. F. and CAMP D. Causes of delays and overruns of construction projects in developing countries. *Proc. CIB, W65 Fourth Symposium*. Waterloo, 1984.
42. MORRELL D. *Indictment, power and politics in the construction industry*. Faber & Faber, London, 1987.
43. EDMUNDS G. A. The construction industry in developing countries. *International Labour Review*, 1979, **118**, No. 3.
44. ARBDALLA M. H. and COCKFIELD R. W. Implementation of capital projects in developing countries: problems and potential solutions. *Proc. CIB, W65 Fourth Symposium*. Waterloo, 1984.
45. MORGAN P. K. and KAMIL M. H. Contract arrangements in the third world. Issues in Engineering. *Journal of Professional Activities, Am. Soc. Civ. Engs, Division of Construction*, 1982, **108**, No. 1 E14.
46. BRISCOE G. *Economics of the construction industry*. Mitchell, London, 1988.
47. VENUS D. H. M. (URRY S. and SHERRATT A. (eds.).) *International construction*. Construction Press, Lancaster, 1980.
48. PAULING G. *The chronicles of a contractor* (reprint). Books of Rhodesia Publishing Co. (PVT) Ltd., 1969.

REFERENCES

49. RANKO B. The world building market. *Proc. CIB, W65 6th Symp.*, Sydney, 1990.
50. THE ECONOMIST. *Economic focus on developing countries*, 11 Dec. 1993.
51. THE ECONOMIST. *A survey of Asia*. 30 Oct. 1993.
52. KELLY J. B. *Arabia, the Gulf and the West*. Harper Collins, London, 1975.
53. EDMONDS G. A. and MILES D. *Foundations for change*. Intermediate Technology Publications, London, 1984.
54. BOUSTEAD H. *The wind of morning*. Chatto & Windus, London, 1975.
55. IMBERT I. D. Human issues affecting construction in developing countries. *Journal of Construction Management and Economics*, 1990, **8**.
56. WELLS J. *The construction industry in developing countries*. Croome Helm, London, 1986.
57. STALLWORTHY E. A. and KHARBANDA O. P. *International construction and the role of project management*. Gower, Aldershot, 1985.
58. TRY H. and REISH M. The experiences of a medium-sized construction company in the Middle East. *Proc. Instn. Civ. Engrs Conf. Management of International Construction Projects*. Thomas Telford, 1984.
59. MURRAY J. *Briefing as a client function*. University of Reading, 1990.
60. POWELL N. C. *Marketing the construction services; review of attitudes and practices*. University of London, unpublished MSc thesis, 1980.
61. BAKER B. N. *et al. Factors affecting project success*. In (CLELLAND D. and KING I. (eds).) *Handbook of project management*. Van Nostran Reinhold, London, 1988.
62. PETERS T. and WATERMAN J. *In search of excellence*. Harper and Row, London, 1982.
63. NEO R. B. *International construction*. Gower, Aldershot, 1976.
64. AYRES D. M. The middle order contractor overseas. *ICE Management of large capital projects*. London, 1978.
65. FLANAGAN R. *et al. A fresh look at the UK and US construction industries*. Building Employers Federation, London, 1986.
66. JONES C. Durgapur steel project. *Indian Construction News*, 1959, .
67. LAING SIR MAURICE. The market—opportunities and risks *in overseas construction opportunities in the construction sector*. Discussion paper 5, National Economic Development Office, London, 1986.
68. FLANAGAN R. *Change the system*. Building, London, 1981.
69. COMPSTON D. G. Discussion contribution *Proc. Instn. Civ. Engrs*

Conf. Management of International Construction Projects. Thomas Telford, London, 1984.

70. VAN HELDEN H. J. Civil engineering and changing transportation concepts in developing countries. *ICE Civil Engineering problems overseas.* Thomas Telford, London, 1971.

71. COCKBURN C. *Construction in overseas development.* Research Publication Services, London, 1970.

72. ROWLAND V. R. Road construction and the consultants' role. *Seminar of National Highways Board.* Pakistan, 1984.

73. MARSH P. D. V. The Dubai aluminium smelter project. *ICE Management of large capital projects.* London, 1978.

74. ROSEVEAR D. A. Financial considerations in overseas projects. *ICE Management of large capital projects.* London, 1978.

75. THOMAS J. M. Managing a contract in a developing country. *ICE Management of large capital projects.* London, 1978.

76. BILLIERE P. DE LA. *Storm command.* Harper Collins, London, 1992.

77. DAMACHI V. G. *Theories of management and the executive in the developing world.* Macmillan, London, 1978.

78. O'CALLAGHAN J. M. *Managerial characteristics and financial performance of construction companies.* Brunel University, unpublished MSc thesis, 1986.

79. GOBELI D. H. and LARSEN E. W. Project structure versus project success. *Project Management Institute, 18th Seminar.* Montreal, 1986.

80. CHERNS A. R. and BRYANT D. T. Studying the client's role in construction management. *Construction Management and Economics,* 1984, **2**.

81. LANGFORD D. A. *Management principals workbook MT2.* University of Bath, 1991.

82. BRITISH STANDARDS INSTITUTE. *Quality systems—model for quality assurance in design, development and production, installation and servicing.* BS 5750, London.

83. BUILDING RESEARCH ESTABLISHMENT. *Quality control on building sites.* London, 1981.

84. FINANCIAL TIMES. *Book review.* Dec. 1993, London.

85. LIESNER T. *One hundred years of economic statistics.* Economist Publications, London, 1989.